WINDOWS
ON *Easter*

Books by Bill Crowder

Overcoming Life's Struggles
The Path of His Passion
Singing the Songs of the Brokenhearted
The Spotlight of Faith
Windows on Christmas

WINDOWS
ON *Easter*

BILL CROWDER

Discovery House®
from Our Daily Bread Ministries

Discovery House is affiliated with
Our Daily Bread Ministries, Grand Rapids, Michigan.

Requests for permission to quote from this book should be
directed to: Permissions Department, Discovery House,
P.O. Box 3566, Grand Rapids, MI 49501 or
contact us by e-mail at permissionsdept@dhp.org.

Scripture taken from the NEW AMERICAN STANDARD
BIBLE®, Copyright © 1960, 1962, 1963, 1968, 1971, 1972,
1973, 1975, 1977, 1995 by The Lockman Foundation.
Used by permission.

Interior Design by Sherri L. Hoffman

Printed in the United States of America

Sixth printing in 2016

For

*Linda and John, Rob and Janice, David and Dina,
Carole and Wes, Kathy and Tim, Scott and Mary Kay*

*Our times lived together have brought their own unique windows
to the experience of life—and to knowing Christ. Thanks.*

CONTENTS

꒰

ACKNOWLEDGMENTS

ow do you ever thank so many for so much? I find myself so thoroughly indebted to all those who have contributed to this project that it is hard to know where to start. My friends, colleagues, and brothers and sisters in Christ at Discovery House Publishers are a priceless treasure. Carol Holquist and the team are remarkable in the way they come alongside an author to help his book be the best he can make it. Judy Markham offers wisdom and patience, and I need large quantities of both from an editor. Annette Gysen has helped shepherd this project through the challenges of the editorial fixes and checks and is always a joy to work with. The DHP crew of Melissa Wade, Katy Pent, Jillian Lamberson, Peg Willison, Kevin Williams, Ed Rock, and Dave Branon is a serious gift. Thank you.

To my family, who have always been encouraging as I try to tackle these writing projects, I just can't say enough. Marlene, my child-bride of over thirty years, is the life partner that has endured the journey without complaint, but with patience, understanding, and love. Our kids (Matt, Beth, Steve, Andy, Mark) and their families are a source of both blessing and reality—and great joy.

This book I also share with my brothers and sisters. As we have grown up and gone our separate ways, I have learned wonderful and valued lessons about character, competition, and comradeship from each of you. I am deeply grateful to be one of you.

In the end, however, it is ultimately an immeasurable honor to be allowed to write about the most momentous events in human history—and to honor the Christ who willingly entered those events for the world—and for me.

INTRODUCTION

γ

hen I wrote *Windows on Christmas* a couple of years ago, my goal was to try to see the familiar through the eyes of the witnesses—both those we would expect, and some who are unexpected. It was a terrific learning experience for me because I have a great fear of the kind of over-familiarity that can jade us and cause us to lose the wonder of the mystery of God.

If that was true of the Christmas story, however, it is that times ten for the events of the Savior's passion. Those moments that opened eternity for the undeserving at the cost of the life of the One who is eternally worthy must be given ascendancy in our hearts and lives; of all events, these must never be allowed to grow stale.

So to try to keep these events fresh in our hearts as we contemplate the death and resurrection of Jesus, I thought it might be useful once again to view those times through the different perspectives of eyewitnesses. Some will be more familiar and others less familiar—but each will have something to say to us.

The old spiritual asks the haunting question of the events surrounding the suffering and victory of Christ:

"Were you there?" These men and women *were* there. We would do well to see what they saw and feel what they felt—that we might be able to learn what they learned. As we look at our Lord's passion through the windows of their various perspectives, may the grace and mercy of Christ grasp our hearts in ways that transform us deeply—like they transformed those who were there.

THE WINDOW *of* SURPRISE

Malchus

The setting for *Master and Commander: The Far Side of the World*, is the South Pacific during the Napoleonic wars of the early 1800s. Captain Jack Aubrey, commander of the British frigate HMS *Surprise*, is battling the much larger and much better armed French warship *Acheron*. As he is preparing for the coming battle, he sets a trap—he dresses the crew as whalers and makes the *Surprise* appear to be a wounded and vulnerable whaling ship instead of a British warship. A *Surprise* indeed!

In Aubrey's final instructions to his men, he challenges them with thoughts of home, reminding them, "England is under threat of invasion. And though we be on the far side of the world, this ship is our home. This ship is England. So it's every hand to his rope or gun. Quick's the word and sharp's the action." He then closes his exhortation with tongue firmly planted in cheek: "After all, *Surprise* is on our side." The men of the HMS *Surprise* respond with uproarious laughter at Aubrey's play on words.

Surprise is that way. It is, well, surprising. And it can be interesting. Sometimes surprises are wonderful and thrilling—like the person who works hard at her job with no expectation of reward or recognition but is surprised with a coveted promotion. The worker often exhibits joyful shock with an ear-to-ear grin that stays plastered on her face for days and days. What a great surprise!

There are other times, however, when surprises can be heartbreaking and even terrifying—like the person who goes in for a routine health checkup feeling great, only to hear the doctor say that there are some serious health problems that need to be addressed. This is, perhaps, one of the worst kinds of surprises.

Surprises, whether good or bad, have the potential to knock us back a little. They challenge our comfortable presuppositions about life. Jesus Christ revealed God to us in one of the most surprising events of history: His incarnation. He was the King and Creator, but He came in poverty. He was holiness personified, yet He reached down to the lowest of the low, even to what this world considered the worst of sinners. Even though He had the power of the universe at His disposal, He chose to yield himself to the tortures of the rebellious world He had come to rescue. None of that was expected from Messiah. He went farther than the people of His day, or our day, could anticipate. He takes us to the edge of the universe and allows us a glimpse inside the throne room of the Father, and what we see there is likely to be far more wonderful and unsettling than we expect. We have a fresh understanding that is filled with surprise.

Surprises abound in the moments surrounding the passion of our Lord, and their impact on the people involved was quite powerful. So many shocking events occurred during those days and nights of pain and darkness and defeat and victory, with an especially compelling incident taking place in Gethsemane the night before the cross. And of all the people surprised by the events that would occur as Christ suffered and died for the sins of the world, I would argue that among those most surprised was Malchus.

WHO WAS THE SURPRISED MAN?

One of the intriguing elements of the story of Christ's passion is how, like in many of history's events, it blends together the famous and the infamous, the heroic and the notorious. Keeping that in mind, it is interesting to note what happens when this little-known chap named Malchus steps onto the stage of history's greatest drama—the events surrounding the death and resurrection of the Son of God. I would argue, however, that, along with Simon Peter, Malchus would have some of the most vivid, most personal, memories of that week.

We see Malchus in what could be described as the trigger for all of the events that would follow—the arrest of Jesus in the garden of Gethsemane. Malchus' story appears in all four of the Gospels (Matthew 26:51–54; Mark 14:47–50; Luke 22:47–53; John 18:10–12), but only the apostle John names him. In fact, it is entirely possible that John not only named Malchus but knew him personally as well. John (who in his gospel regularly refers to himself as an unnamed disciple, or the "disciple that Jesus loved") describes himself (John 18:15) as "known to the high priest." It is not at all a stretch to think that someone known *to* the high priest would be known *by* Malchus, the servant of the high priest (John uses the definite article *the* to show a very specific role for Malchus in the household of Caiaphas, the high priest).

In the Gospels where Malchus is not named, however, he is described. Each of the gospel records refers to him as the servant or slave of the high priest. In each case, the word used is the Greek term *doulos*. This word was used for a class of slaves in the first century who were bonded to their master. What did that mean? *Smith's Bible Dictionary* describes a couple of the situations in which a Hebrew man would become a slave in ancient Israel:

- He may have lost his property and was unable to support his family, so he might sell himself, hoping that he might one day be able to earn enough to redeem his property.
- A convicted thief would become a slave until he could work off the value of the restitution money he owed.

While the life of a *doulos* was normally a tolerable life for a Hebrew, it was not a life of freedom, promise, or opportunity. And now Malchus, the servant of the high priest, one who did not know freedom, was on his way to Christ's garden of prayer to try to capture the One who had come to free men's souls. Adding to the irony, the name Malchus means "king or kingdom" (*Smith's Bible Dictionary*).

The slave whose name meant "king" was coming to arrest the King who had come to serve, not to be served (Mark 10:45). Fascinating—and surprising.

As Malchus arrived at the garden, however, he was far from alone. William Barclay, in his commentary on John's gospel, wrote about the group that came to arrest Jesus:

> There is something astonishing about the force which came out to arrest Jesus. John said that there was a company of soldiers, together with officers from the chief priests and Pharisees. The *officers* would be Temple police. The Temple authorities had a kind of private police force to keep good order, and the Sanhedrin had its police officers to carry out its decrees. The officers, therefore, were the Jewish police force. But there was a band of Roman soldiers there, too. The word is *speira*. Now that word, if it is correctly used, can have three meanings. It is the Greek word for a Roman cohort and a cohort of 600 men. If it was a cohort of auxiliary soldiers, speira had one thousand men, two hundred and forty cavalry and seven hundred and sixty infantry. Sometimes, much more rarely the word is used for the detachment of men called a maniple which was made up of two hundred men.
>
> Even if we take this word to mean the smallest force, the maniple, what an expedition to send out against an unarmed Galilean carpenter!

And so, into the stillness of the garden where the disciples have been sleeping and Jesus has been praying, an army erupts—and at the front of the line is Malchus.

WHAT THE SURPRISED MAN EXPERIENCED

An old country preacher I heard long ago liked to say, "Some lessons are better felt than tell't." While the preacher's grammar may be suspect, it is a truism that experience often serves as one of life's great teachers. Howard Hendricks, the Dallas Seminary professor who has shaped so many pastors' ministries, said, "If teaching were telling, my children would be geniuses." It's true. The lessons of life we most clearly remember tend to be the ones we experience—particularly when that experience is accompanied by pain.

When I was in the tenth grade, I came home from school one afternoon and told my mom that I was heading back out to play football at a friend's house. She made it clear, in no uncertain terms, that I wasn't going anywhere until I had done my homework. However, while she wasn't looking, I slipped out the backdoor to go play in spite of her instructions. We played until dinnertime, but, on the final play, I was tackled into my friend's swing set—and broke my front tooth. That injury resulted in over twenty years and thousands of dollars worth of dental problems and a painful and expensive lesson in the consequences of disobedience that I will never forget. I didn't hear about it—I experienced it!

Malchus' encounter with Christ would also be marked by the experience of pain—but not at the hands of Jesus. Rather, his pain came at the hands of one of Jesus' men.

Attacked by Peter

> Simon Peter then, having a sword, drew it and struck the high priest's slave, and cut off his right ear; and the slave's name was Malchus (John 18:10).

Peter's foolish attack on Malchus is found in all four gospel records, but only John's record names Peter. Bible scholars speculate that because John was writing long after Peter had died, there was no longer any danger in naming him as the one who attacked the Roman troops (an act of sedition), whereas the other gospel records were written while Peter still lived. We don't know for sure why only John gives us the name of the fisherman as the attacker, but, in an incident full of surprises, it isn't exactly a surprise that Simon Peter would be the perpetrator. Simon, the most impulsive of the disciples, steps out of the fearful band of Christ-followers and swings his sword. One Bible teacher said that it is obvious that Peter was a fisherman and not a soldier, because he undoubtedly was swinging for Malchus' head and missed—getting only an ear.

Bible commentator William Hendriksen offered three descriptions of Peter's attack on Malchus, and none were particularly positive:

- Unprofitable—because it could not accomplish the desired goal
- Unnecessary—because the Father was more than capable of protecting His Son
- Unenlightened—because the attack failed to reckon the message of the bread and the cup Jesus had just shared with the apostles in the upper room: Jesus must be arrested in order to be killed, in order to truly be "the Lamb of God who takes away the sins of the world."

Still, lest we beat Peter up too much, we need to see something that is both noble and courageous about his attack. In this ill-advised and ultimately futile act we nevertheless see Peter trying to keep his promise to Jesus. On the road to Gethsemane, after Jesus and His men had left the upper room where they had celebrated the last supper, Jesus told them that they would all forsake Him and flee. Peter, however, committed to stand firm:

> But Peter said to Him, "Even though all may fall away because of You, I will never fall away." Jesus said to him, "Truly I say to you that this very night, before a rooster crows, you will deny Me three times." Peter said to Him, "Even if I have to die

with You, I will not deny You." All the disciples said
the same thing too (Matthew 26:33–35).

Now, confronted by a huge force and armed with a single blade, Peter nevertheless waded into the mob—genuinely
willing to give his life for the Master. For Peter, it was a foolish action, but I think it was also a brave one. I suspect he
deserves a little more credit here than we usually give him.

For Malchus, however, it was a moment of sheer terror.
Standing at the head of a small army, he went from a position of power to a condition of agony in a split second. What
would happen to him? Would he bleed to death? Would he
survive? For the servant of the high priest, an event full of
surprises has evolved into a real shock. The entire troop
must have wanted to retaliate against the Galilean and His
men for this action.

Healed by Jesus

But Jesus answered and said, "Stop! No more
of this." And He touched his ear and healed him
(Luke 22:51).

Interestingly, only Luke, the physician, mentions the
healing in his gospel. Hendriksen points out in his commentary that Luke stays true to his profession as a doctor
and not only records the healing Jesus performs but also
mentions that it was Malchus' *right* ear that was lopped off.
Hendriksen says:

Had the ear been slashed off and was it hanging by a shred of skin? However one conceives of this, Luke, himself a healer, reports that Jesus touched the man's ear and healed him. It must not be possible for anyone to repeat truthfully that Jesus has either himself done anything wrong or has permitted it to remain uncorrected when done by someone else. Besides we once more see Jesus as the Great Sympathizer and Healer, the Savior, and this not only of the soul (in the case of all who put their trust in him) but even for the body.

James Montgomery Boice agrees, "Surely the greatest truth of this incident is that Jesus was here showing mercy even to his enemies, and this even at the time they came to thrust him toward his execution."

Confused by Both?

I can only begin to imagine the confusion this rapid-fire series of events must have caused in the heart and mind of this poor servant, Malchus. He was completely and thoroughly unprepared for these events! Attacked by a fisherman? Healed by the man he had come to arrest? How could he even begin to process these things?

The event must have set Malchus' mind spinning. *How could someone I was trying to harm show such compassion to me? Who is this Jesus after all?* He had heard, no doubt, the deliberations of Caiaphas and his cronies as they plotted and strategized to arrest Jesus. He perhaps even agreed with the accusation that this man was a threat to the nation. But now this man had healed him. His healed right ear was proof of something, wasn't it? Could it be that his master, Caiaphas, was terribly wrong about the one the Galilean disciples called master? After a night of surprises, poor Malchus, I am convinced, was now overwhelmed—he had experienced more than he could process. More than he could understand. More than he could ever explain to Caiaphas.

WHAT THE SURPRISED MAN HEARD

While experience can teach us, experience by itself will always fall short of our deepest heart needs. It will always feel keenly inadequate because we long for truth to bring clarity and context to the life experiences that so dramatically impact us. This truth is demonstrated in the Gethsemane experience of Malchus, the servant of the high priest. Shocked by the attack, surprised by the healing, he needed to have a frame of reference for what had happened to him. He needed to understand who this person that he had come to arrest was, this one who had healed him.

In the biblical record, this man who had lost his ear would, upon his miraculous healing at Christ's hand, be exposed to extraordinary truth as the Savior responded to His arrest and the events that would follow. As he heard the Master's words through a freshly repaired ear, Malchus was exposed to four profound truths.

Truth #1: The Plan of the Father

[Jesus said], "Put your sword back into its place; for all those who take up the sword shall perish by the sword. Or do you think that I cannot appeal to My Father, and He will at once put at My disposal more than twelve legions of angels? How then will the Scriptures be fulfilled, which say that it must happen this way?" (Matthew 26:52–54).

Arriving at the garden to participate in the arrest of the itinerant preacher that had caused his master so much consternation, Malchus had to have believed that it was Caiaphas who was orchestrating the events of that evening. Malchus must have been shocked and awed, however, as Jesus makes it abundantly clear that it is none other than God the Father himself—not Caiaphas—whose purposes were being accomplished.

Truth #2: The Irony of the Arrest

And Jesus said to them, "Have you come out with swords and clubs to arrest Me, as you would against a robber? Every day I was with you in the temple teaching, and you did not seize Me; but this has taken place to fulfill the Scriptures" (Mark 14:48–49).

How bizarre it must have seemed that the Christ, who had been open and public in His teaching in the temple, would be arrested in private in a garden. What a strange reaction on the part of the authorities, that even though they believed that the one they sought was a fraud and a charlatan, they were sufficiently fearful to enlist an army to ensure a successful arrest! As Jesus drew attention to these ironies, Malchus must have wondered why an army would have been ordered, under the cover of night, to arrest a man who would defend and heal an enemy.

Truth #3: The Hour of Darkness

> Then Jesus said to the chief priests and officers of the temple and elders who had come against Him, "Have you come out with swords and clubs as you would against a robber? While I was with you daily in the temple, you did not lay hands on Me; but this hour and the power of darkness are yours" (Luke 22:52–53).

I wonder how it must have seemed to Malchus to have come on this mission, no doubt with a charge from Caiaphas himself. To come believing he had a part in protecting Israel. To come to arrest a threat to the nation. Yet having been miraculously healed by the alleged criminal, he is now told that, in fact, he is not part of an army of light—but a representative of the power and hour of darkness.

Truth #4: The Cup That Awaits

So Jesus said to Peter, "Put the sword into the sheath; the cup which the Father has given Me, shall I not drink it?" (John 18:11).

Jesus was reminding Peter of the upper room, the Passover, and the cup He would take for himself. The cup the Father gave Jesus was the cup of suffering that the cross embodied, the cup for which Christ, on the cross, would thirst (John 19:28). Yet while everything human in us leads us to self-defense and self-protection, Jesus orders Peter to sheath his sword.

With that, the disciples flee for their lives, and Malchus and his army arrest the solitary Galilean and lead Him away to His awaiting cross. Following the arrest of Jesus, Malchus is never mentioned again in the Bible, leaving us with frustrated questions:

- What was the long-range impact of the surprising events of that night?
- Did Malchus feel remorse for leading his Healer to trial and death?
- Would Malchus ever be made spiritually whole by the Savior who had made him physically whole?

In *The Life of Christ: A Study Guide to the Gospel Record*, M. S. Mills wrote, "The fact that his name was given six decades after the event suggests that he was well known to the initial readers of John (his name does not appear again in the New Testament), so this may indicate that he did indeed place his faith in Jesus as the Messiah."

I love that idea—but we just don't know. What we do know, however, is that for the rest of his life, Malchus wore on the right side of his head the proof of an encounter with the God-man. For the rest of his life, whenever he heard the name of Jesus, his hand must have unconsciously moved to touch that restored right ear. For the rest of his life, he would be unable to deny the love and care that he had experienced in what one poet called "the touch of the Master's hand." For the rest of his life, he bore the evidence of the greatest surprise he would ever experience.

Boris Pasternak, the author of *Doctor Zhivago*, said, "Surprise is the greatest gift which life can grant us." If that is true, then perhaps no one has ever received a more precious gift of surprise than our friend, Malchus. Charles Morgan said, "There is no surprise more magical than the surprise of being loved: It is God's finger on man's shoulder." Malchus knew what it was to be owned, and, as a result of Peter's behavior, knew what it was to be hated. In Christ, however, he had known what it was to be cared for and loved. That had to have been a surprise, given the nature of the circumstances under which he met the Savior.

I would suggest that if we are honest enough with ourselves about our true nature, God's expressions of love and care for us should surprise us as well. After all, these things are true of us, as they were of Malchus:

- It was not after we made ourselves good enough that God loved us.
- It was not after we got our act together that God loved us.
- It was not after we had sufficiently cleaned up our lives that God loved us.

Paul reminds us, "But God demonstrates His own love toward us, in that while we were yet sinners, Christ died for us" (Romans 5:8).

While we were yet sinners... Now *that* is a surprise.

THE WINDOW of SIN

Judas Iscariot

One of my favorite expressions is the term *everyman*. It suggests those things that are regular, average, and normal. In fact, the definition of *everyman* is itself undistinguished; the *Merriam-Webster Collegiate Dictionary* simply says "the typical or ordinary person." *Everyman's* idiom equivalent is "the man in the street." Being pretty average myself, I warm to these ideas, for they remind me that *average* means "average" because that is where most of us land on the sliding scale of humanity. Let the world have its remarkable and outstanding and fabulous folk (we probably need them, too). *Everyman* is the word that belongs to me and all the other average people in the world, and I embrace it wholeheartedly.

However, there are moments when the average person steps into a role in history that is far beyond average. Times when the ordinary must, however uncomfortably, wear the mantle of the extraordinary. This happens when an "everyman" makes the choice to walk a path that is not at all ordinary. Despite the unremarkable nature of an everyman's background, he or she can make choices that have astounding results for good or evil, shaping lives and even history. Two such "everymen" who marked history from very different directions were:

- An unremarkable young corporal in the army. Quiet and aloof, raised by religious parents, he was a failed artist who harbored the pain of rejection and even imprisonment before turning within and finding reason to hate and to kill. He determined that all of his problems were ultimately the fault of the Jews—and rose to a position where he could murder them by the millions, for no greater reason than his own personal hatred. This everyman? Adolf Hitler.

- An accomplished watchmaker, this man built a home, a business, and a family during the most difficult of times. Shaped by his faith rather than just being branded by it, his religious convictions would not allow him to watch the world and stay silent about what he saw. He could not be content with protecting himself and his own but made the choice to, at great risk, provide rescue for others. He developed a way to hide the Jews escaping the Nazi death camps in his own home, knowing that it could (and did) cost him his life and family. This everyman? Corrie ten Boom's father, Casper ten Boom.

Two everymen—both faced with options. Both shaped their own futures and eternities (and those of others) by how they responded to the pressures of the day. One is lesser known, but his name is associated with the courage of his choice to rescue. The other would bring only shame to his name—forever.

You see, it is here, in the consequences of life's choices, that we see something very significant—for here we come face to face with sin and the power of our choices to corrupt, to distract, and to destroy. That power is witnessed in the lives of a variety of "everymen" in the Bible, but it is made especially clear in the life of Judas, the everyman who betrayed the Lord Jesus Christ, bringing shame and dishonor to his name for all eternity because he yielded himself to the power of sin.

THE IDENTITY OF ONE EVERYMAN

Who was this man? What can we know about him? Certainly not enough to fully unravel the thought processes and choices that led to his downfall—but perhaps enough to give us some kind of frame of reference for at least trying to understand him and what he did. What do we know of him?

His Name. Judas (which means "praised") was a name that had all the elements of nobility. It was ultimately derived from the ancient name of Judah, who was one of the sons of Jacob/Israel. It was Judah's idea to sell his brother Joseph into slavery to preserve his own position in Jacob's family, but years later he offered himself as a slave in place of Benjamin, the youngest brother, showing that he had experienced a remarkable heart transformation. When the aged Jacob gave blessings to his sons, he declared that Judah's line would be the kingly tribe of Israel from which the Messiah would come into the world.

The name *Judas* also brought to mind a hero closer to the first-century era of Judas Iscariot, one of the greatest leaders in Jewish history, Judas Maccabeus—Judas the Hammer. Judas Maccabeus had delivered the nation from the oppression of the Assyrians, restoring the worship of the temple and establishing a mindset of fierce nationalism that would still mark the people of Israel over a hundred years later when the Roman legions arrived in Palestine. The Jewish feast of Hanukkah is still commemorated today as testimony to the courage and devotion of Judas Maccabeus, and the restoration of the temple is celebrated in the Festival of Lights. For Jews, being named Judas in the first century was like an American being named after George Washington. *Judas* was perceived as a heroic, enviable name—but the Judas named Iscariot would change all of that. Now, even in the *Merriam-Webster Collegiate Dictionary, Judas* means "one who betrays under the guise of friendship." No matter how you slice it, that definition is a far cry from "praise." As Matthew Coder wrote, we name our dogs Nero and Caesar, but no one would name even a dog Judas. From honor to shame, the connotation of the name *Judas* has been shaped by the choices of one everyman.

His Family. In John 6:71, Judas is described as "the son of Simon Iscariot." We don't know any more than this. Some have speculated that the Simon here was Simon the tanner, in whose Joppa home Peter had the clean/unclean vision of the sheet of animals coming down from heaven in Acts 10.

His Hometown. Many believe that his full name, Judas Iscariot (Matthew 10:4), hints at the geographic roots of this everyman. *Iscariot* may be translated "Ish (man) Kerioth (Kirjath)" or "man from Kerioth." This is helpful information because there were two cities that began with the name Kirjath, suggesting possible hometowns for this disciple. Of the two, the most likely was south of Jerusalem near Hebron, Kiriath, an Edomite city on the southeast border of Israel and Edom (Joshua 15:25) that was home to many Jews in the first century. Was it Judas' home? Possibly.

It is important to note, however, that others see the title *Iscariot* having a political significance rather than a geographic one. *Harper's Bible Dictionary* affirms both of these possibilities but suggests others as well: "The origin of the name Iscariot is debated. Some suggestions are: man (Hebrew, *ish*) of Karioth; the assassin (from Greek, *sikarios*); man from Issachar. Certainty is impossible, but if the first is correct, Judas was the only apostle from Judea."

The theory that *Iscariot* could find its root in *sicarius* (the assassin) is noteworthy. The word *sicarius* was the name for a small dagger used for murders—especially among the Zealots. If this theory is correct, it may help explain Judas' disappointment that Christ refused to claim the kingdom as His own. If, in fact, Judas was a member of the Zealots, then he advocated the violent overthrow of Roman oppression—something that Jesus continually opposed. This, then, could form the real possibility of a motive for Judas' betrayal of Christ: disappointment in Jesus' refusal to take the kingdom by force. While the evidence that *Iscariot* means "the assassin" is not conclusive, it does have merit and cannot simply be dismissed.

ℑ

THE MINISTRY OF ONE EVERYMAN

Some years ago, American Express had a provocative theme for its advertising campaign: "Membership has its privileges."

The ads suggested the seemingly magical powers of the American Express card to open doors that were otherwise closed to mere mortals and to provide opportunities normally reserved only for the ultra-special. The strategy was to dangle the somewhat secretive privileges of membership in front of ordinary people (the everymen) who, to this point, had not qualified for membership in this very desirable club. The hope was that the unqualified would grasp at this "carrot on a stick," doing whatever was necessary to become qualified. For common folk, it was the allure of that which is just beyond reach—only making it all the more tantalizing. Everyone wanted membership because everyone wanted to share in those wondrous privileges.

Not all privileges come from membership in secret clubs or credit card companies. In fact, it could be argued that the common everymen who traveled with the Son of God during the days of His public ministry experienced the greatest privileges ever. And, as surprising as it may be, Judas shared in all of those privileges! The gospel records do not paint a picture of eleven faithful men and one pariah floating on the fringes of the organization. Far from it. We see Judas more in the role of the ultimate insider, with all the privileges of membership in the most remarkable group ever formed. He was a disciple of Jesus, sharing all the privileges that Peter, James, John, or any of the rest of the apostolic band had. He saw and felt and lived and did things most of us could only dream of. The following are some of the privileges he enjoyed as one who walked with the Messiah.

The Privilege of Exposure. Consider all that Judas saw and heard. Consider all that he was exposed to! For three years he was a close associate of the Son of God. He walked and talked with Jesus; he sat under the stars with Him, broke bread with Him, and listened to Him. Judas heard firsthand the Sermon on the Mount and the parables, with their piercing messages. He saw the blind receive sight, the deaf made to hear, the crippled and diseased wholly healed, the demon-possessed set free. Judas didn't read thirdhand reports about these events—he had a front-row seat for the public ministry of the Son of God. So many times I hear fellow followers of Christ lament, "How I wish I could have walked with Jesus and heard His voice and seen His miracles!" Judas had that privilege, and more as well.

The Privilege of Involvement. Note this account in Luke 10:17–20:

> The seventy returned with joy, saying, "Lord, even the demons are subject to us in Your name." And He said to them, "I was watching Satan fall from heaven like lightning. Behold, I have given you authority to tread on serpents and scorpions, and over all the power of the enemy, and nothing will injure you. Nevertheless do not rejoice in this, that the spirits are subject to you, but rejoice that your names are recorded in heaven."

Amazing. Apparently the seventy was a group of followers of Christ, of which the Twelve was a subset. Like concentric circles, the privilege of involvement with Jesus increased as the circles got smaller. On the outside, perhaps, was the five hundred (1 Corinthians 15:6); then the one hundred and twenty (Acts 1:15); then the seventy; then the Twelve; and ultimately the inner circle of three—Peter, James, and John. Judas was one of the Twelve and, as a result, was part of this group as well. But not only was he part of the group, he fully participated in their activities. As hard as it might be for us to believe about the one who betrayed Jesus, Judas Iscariot cast out demons and worked miracles like the rest. He was not a benchwarmer—Judas was in the game, doing the same ministry work as the other disciples of Jesus. In fact, following Judas' death, Peter would say, "Brethren, the Scripture had to be fulfilled, which the Holy Spirit foretold by the mouth of David concerning Judas, who became a guide to those who arrested Jesus. For he was counted among us and received his share in this ministry" (Acts 1:16–17).

Judas "received his share in this ministry." I find that remarkable.

The Privilege of Responsibility. But there is more. Judas was not only one of the Twelve, he was a trusted member of that group. In fact, he was so trusted that he "had the money box," John 13:29 tells us. That Judas had been chosen to be the treasurer shows that the group had strong confidence in him. Remember, as a tax collector, Matthew would have had a lot of experience in handling money, a set of skills that would have made him a reasonable choice to be the group's treasurer. Apparently, however, Judas had so thoroughly won their trust that he was seen as a man to be respected, a man of character. By common consent, he handled the money, but, "It is required of stewards that one be found trustworthy" (1 Corinthians 4:2). The task of treasurer carries responsibility with it.

A careful study of the Gospels reveals that there was absolutely nothing about Judas that hinted that he would become a traitor. As one of Victorian novelist George Eliot's characters observed, "A perfect traitor should have a face on which vice can write no marks, lips which lie with a dimpled smile, eyes of such agate-like brightness and depth that no infamy can dull them, cheeks that can rise from a murder and not look haggard." Judas was one of the Twelve, and none of the other disciples suspected a thing. Only Jesus knew him as the traitor he would become (John 6:70).

THE TURNING OF ONE EVERYMAN

How did it happen that Judas went from being a man respected and trusted by the other disciples to the one who betrayed Jesus with a kiss? In recent years, some in my generation have chosen to portray Judas as, at best, a misunderstood hero or, at worst, a victim. This certainly seems to be the case in Andrew Lloyd Webber's *Jesus Christ, Superstar,* in which Judas is portrayed in a positive light as a tragic figure, while, at the end of the rock opera, Jesus still hangs on the cross. Contemporary attempts to absolve Judas of any wrongdoing, however, don't hold up against the biblical record. Remember, Jesus called Judas "a devil" and "the son of perdition" (John 6:70; 17:12). What happened? Again, we can't say with certainty, but there is enough information to construct a theory that makes reasonable sense. The downward spiral of Judas' life may have begun with a moment of:

Disenchantment. One of the truly lovely moments in the Gospels occurred at the home of Lazarus, the brother of Mary and Martha. After Jesus had raised Lazarus from the dead, Martha gave a feast in honor of Jesus. A moment of true beauty occurred when Mary, another sister of Lazarus, stepped into the room to anoint Jesus with a fragrant ointment—an extravagant expression of her love and gratitude. As the scent of the perfume hung in the air, however, Judas offered his cynical critique and shattered the wonderful moment in John 12:5: "Why was this perfume not sold for three hundred denarii and given to poor people?" It certainly sounds like a noble idea, until we see the motive behind his words:

> Now he said this, not because he was concerned about the poor, but because he was a thief, and as he had the money box, he used to pilfer what was put into it (John 12:6).

A picture of this man's heart begins to form, and it is likely that, at this point, Judas clearly understood that things were not going to turn out as he had hoped. Judas may have enlisted with the Twelve because he wanted an earthly kingdom and the wealth that kingdom would bring. Now, he was pilfering from the common money box—but may have already realized he would never see what he had longed for. If so, that disenchantment and unrealized desire made Judas a prime candidate for:

Spiritual Failure. Notice two different statements in the Gospels:

- Luke 22:3: "And Satan entered into Judas who was called Iscariot, belonging to the number of the twelve."
- John 13:27: "After the morsel, Satan then entered into [Judas]. Therefore Jesus said to him, 'What you do, do quickly.'"

After three years of walking with the Prince of Light, Judas chose instead the prince of darkness. After walking with the Son of God, Judas made his stand with the enemy of God, and it seems to have occurred in two stages. The Luke 22 passage says that Judas' yielding to Satan led him to go to the chief priests and offer to betray Jesus to them. The John 13 passage, however, takes us right into the upper room, as Judas left Jesus and His men to actually carry out the betrayal that he had planned beforehand with the religious establishment. In both cases, it is a vivid reminder that exposure to spiritual things—even the presence of Christ himself—is not the equivalent of a true relationship with God through His Son. Yet, even in the upper room, before Judas' departure, none imagined him to be the betrayer Jesus spoke of. When Jesus predicted His betrayer, John tells us that they were all "at a loss" to know which of their fellow disciples Jesus was speaking of (13:21). Judas, like the spiritual enemy to whom he had yielded himself, had become darkness but learned to masquerade as light (2 Corinthians 11:14).

Treason. From disenchantment to spiritual failure, Judas now made his decline complete as he led an army into the garden of Gethsemane in order to capture the Christ.

> Immediately Judas went to Jesus and said, "Hail, Rabbi!" and kissed Him (Matthew 26:49).

Plainly seen, the biblical record condemns Judas for the willingness and even the energy with which he betrayed his Master. In *The Path of His Passion,* I described the betrayal in the garden for what it was. The biblical record plainly condemns Judas for the willingness, and even the energy, with which he betrayed his Master:

> Judas' words are masked in hypocrisy as he says, "Hail, Rabbi." This was a common greeting that meant, "I'm so glad to see you!" It was the ultimate in two-faced deception, and he somehow—wrongly—thought that he could get away with it. He then leans forward and "kisses Him." The form of the Greek verb here is strong and emphatic. It means that Judas embraced Jesus and kept on kissing Him. The intensity of the word reveals that Judas did not just betray Jesus—he did so enthusiastically. It is a word that is filled with passion.

We clearly see the rise and fall of Judas Iscariot from faithful follower to energetic betrayer. While Judas' treachery in the garden demands our attention, we also must see something else. Judas' evil kiss may dominate the scene, but we can also plainly see the sacrificial spirit of Jesus.

This sacrificial spirit is brilliantly captured in Caravaggio's classic painting *The Taking of Christ.* While travelling in Dublin, Ireland, my wife Marlene and I visited the National Gallery, where the most famous painting on display is this masterpiece by Caravaggio. We searched the entire museum until we finally found it, and it was worth the effort. The painting was as breathtaking as it was huge, portraying the darkness of Judas' betrayal and the tragedy of his spiritual failure. However, no sooner are viewers' eyes drawn to the act of the traitor's kiss than they are pulled lower on the canvas to see the hands of Jesus—passively held in front of Him to show that He was offering no resistance to the arrest—the One who went quietly, "as a lamb that is led to slaughter" (Isaiah 53:7). The One who said, "No one can take my life from me. I sacrifice it voluntarily" (John 10:18 NLT).

Ironically, the man named Judah betrayed the Lion of the tribe of Judah—and the Lion gave himself up like a lamb. Where did it all begin? For Judas, it may have been something as seemingly innocent as becoming a little disgruntled, a little dissatisfied—but what a dangerous thing. Judas probably never expected that his seemingly minor complaints would be his first steps on the path to becoming a traitor. No wonder God judged Israel so harshly for murmuring in the wilderness. Judas' example explains why one of the things God hates is "one who sows discord amon brethren" (Proverbs 6:19 NKJV). The result is always destructive. And the result was certainly destructive for a once-trusted, active, committed disciple who turned into a hated, vilified, shamed traitor who betrayed his friend with a kiss. Can it be any different for you or me?

THE END OF ONE EVERYMAN

The 1971 movie *Brian's Song* (about Chicago Bear football players Brian Piccolo and Gale Sayers) began with the narrator telling the audience, "Every true story ends in death. This is a true story." The Judas story is also a true story, and it likewise ends in death. If you are like me, you always want stories to have a happy ending, but there is no joy in the conclusion of Judas' story. It is a dark symphony, played in a minor key, and developed in three movements:

Regret: Having received a payment of thirty pieces of silver (ironically, the price of a slave) for his agreement to betray Jesus, Judas completed the deed—but suffered regret for it afterward. He returned to the temple leaders and tried to give back the money, "saying, 'I have sinned by betraying innocent blood'" (Matthew 27:4). Sadly, while the Bible says that Judas felt remorse (Matthew 27:3), it does not say he actually repented and sought forgiveness from the God he had betrayed. Without forgiveness to heal his guilty heart, his only option was escape.

Self-destruction: In Matthew 27:1–10, the story of Judas' self-destruction unfolds, with the ultimate display of Judas' despair reflected in the simple statement of verse 5: "and he went away and hanged himself." The guilt of his betrayal fully bore down on him, and Judas (unlike Peter, whose betrayal of Jesus took the form of denials rather than a kiss) chose death over repentance. In death, however, Judas would find no relief. Instead, he would find only judgment.

Judgment: In Acts 1:25, Luke tells us that Judas' ultimate end was not at the end of a rope. It was the place of judgment. Luke says that Judas, in death, went to "his own place"—understood by Bible scholars to mean a Christless eternity. It implies that, like the rich man Jesus spoke of in the story of Lazarus the beggar, Judas immediately lifted up his eyes in torment, having arrived at the eternal destiny his choices demanded.

What destroyed Judas? Fate, sovereignty, circumstances of life? No. At the end of the day, Judas was destroyed by the power of sin, a power seen clearly in the self-destructive choices he had made in his own life.

The story is told of an artist who was commissioned to paint a Sicilian cathedral with a mural depicting the life of Jesus. He discovered a twelve-year-old boy whose radiant innocence made a perfect model for the Christ child. Years later, it was

Passion Week, and the artist had completed all the major figures except Judas. One day, a man whose face showed the results of years of alcohol abuse staggered into a tavern where the artist was sitting. Immediately the artist chose him to be the model for Judas. Leading the man to the cathedral, he pointed to the bare space on the wall and asked him to pose as Judas. The derelict broke down into sobs, "Don't you remember me?" Pointing to the Christ child, the man explained, "Many years ago, I was your model for Him."

Bible teacher Leslie Flynn wrote,

> The story of Judas is often repeated. A person can be numbered with the people of God, serve on church boards, be active on committees, take communion, but go out to covetous practice and raw business deals, and at last to a lost eternity— right from church. Even after associating with Christ and His followers, we can harbor a devil in our hearts. Though no one is asked today to deliver Christ bodily into enemy hands, nevertheless people do betray Him in more subtle ways.

The byproduct of sin is that it destroys without mercy. Our destruction does not demand that we betray Jesus with a kiss, as long as we betray Him with our lives. Of this, one poet wrote:

> It may not be for silver, it may not be for gold
> But yet by tens of thousands the Prince of life is sold.

Judas Iscariot

Sold for a godless friendship, sold for a selfish aim
Sold for a fleeting trifle, sold for an empty name.
Sold in the mart of science, sold in the seat of power
Sold at the shrine of fortune, sold at pleasure's bower
Sold—for your awful bargain none but God can see—
Ponder my soul the question, shall He be sold by
    Thee?
Sold! O God what a moment! Stilled is the conscience
    voice,
Sold! and a weeping angel records the fateful choice,
Sold! but the price accepted to a living coal shall
    turn,
With the pangs of a late repentance deep in the soul
    to burn.

        (In Herbert Lockyer, *All the Apostles of the Bible*)

THE WINDOW *of* SIGNIFICANCE

The Centurion

Through the centuries, soldiers have been figures either despised or revered—despised by those they come to conquer and revered by those they protect and defend. We are often shocked at the actions war (itself a result of hatred and sin) forces them to take—yet we are frequently amazed by the courage it requires for soldiers to take those actions. Those of us who have never experienced the horror of combat cannot comprehend the toll a soldier's work takes on him or her. Although we can't fully understand, we appreciate the significant sacrifices soldiers make for us, so every year at Memorial Day we stand and cheer and applaud and shed tears of appreciation for what soldiers have endured for our safety and protection.

Endured. Yes, that is the right word. The soldier's task is far from easy and often extremely unpleasant. Soldiers suffer the hardships of training and are often subjected, in combat, to a lifestyle of deprivation. It is a life that often seems barely civilized, alternating between acts of valor and barbarism. The soldier's life is also an existence filled with fear and danger—especially because many times the soldier doesn't know where danger is coming from.

The story is told of an order sent at the outbreak of World War I from headquarters in London to a British outpost in Africa. The order read, "We are at war. Arrest all foreigners." A short time later, the outpost sent the following response to HQ, "We have arrested ten Germans, six Belgians, four Frenchmen, two Italians, three Austrians, and an American. Please advise immediately who we're at war with." While humorous, that story nevertheless reminds us that part of the terror of war is its unpredictability. And that is a fearful thing, indeed.

There is another frightening aspect to life as a soldier, however, and that is the constant reality of being faced with death; this reality often leads to what is known as "foxhole prayers"—desperate cries to God, even from soldiers who aren't always convinced God is there. To live continually in the shadow of death is a difficult thing, to say the least. The other difficult aspect of death for soldiers is somehow reconciling the reality that they are agents of death. Being forced to take another's life, even for a just cause, can be difficult to live with.

The life of a soldier is not an easy life. It isn't now—and it wasn't two thousand years ago either. Yet, even lives and hearts forged in the heat of battles and the struggles of military service are not beyond the reach of the gospel. In fact, no person is stronger than the power of the cross. We see the impact of this power in the life of a soldier, a person of significance who, in turn, declared the significance of the Christ. The soldier in question? The centurion in charge of the crucifixion of Jesus Christ.

A CENTURION'S LIFE

Our oldest son is in the Army, and he has been a soldier now for several years. Watching him progress through the ranks from recruit to basic trainee to private to private first class to corporal to sergeant to staff sergeant has been an education in what life in the military is like. In many ways, I feel certain that the core elements of soldiering have not changed appreciably over the centuries. Certainly the technology has changed, and the training is more advanced. The basic tasks, however, are not so dissimilar. Soldiers are committed to putting the mission before comfort, their comrades before self, and obedience to duty above their personal opinions about the orders they are given. It is a lifestyle rooted in discipline, authority structures, and teamwork. What might military life have looked like for a first-century Roman centurion?

The Position of a Centurion. The word *centurion* comes from the Latin term *centum*, meaning "one hundred." A centurion was a Roman officer in command of a hundred men. In order to have a proper grasp of a centurion's role, it may be useful to understand the design of a Roman legion. History tells us:

- each legion was divided into ten cohorts
- each cohort into three maniples, and
- each maniple into two centuries

If we do the math, we see that in a legion there were thirty maniples and sixty centuries. A *century* always consisted of a hundred soldiers, meaning that sixty centuries would form a combined legion of some six thousand troops. The centurion? In the scheme of the Roman army, he would have had the role of "top sergeant"—generally considered the most critical role in the chain of command to the success of any military operation. The generals may plan the strategies and decide the tactics, but it is the top sergeant who has to make that plan succeed on the ground, and the same was true for the centurion.

The office of centurion was the highest rank an ordinary soldier could achieve, and the position was similar to what we know as a company commander, according to *Harper's Bible Dictionary*. Sixty centurions would serve each legion, and there were grades among those sixty, with the highest ranking centurion holding a position that would be the equivalent of a knight among Roman nobility. Promotion to the office of centurion was usually based on experience and knowledge, and in the Roman army, just as in the military today, centurions would be promoted as they transferred to positions of increasing responsibility.

The centurion earned his position the hard way, but it was a position of prestige and honor, commanding the respect of others. Centurions would receive substantial pensions at retirement and would be viewed as notables in the towns where they lived. The centurions of Luke 7 and Acts 10 were obviously men of financial means who contributed to their communities and were respected by them.

The Life of a Warrior. Again, it was not easy to gain the position of centurion. While some were able to purchase their rank as centurion and some were appointed because they were favored by higher ranking officers or Roman officials, centurions were most often appointed by the tribunes over them. These promotions were almost always based on a soldier's merit, with good conduct being a key consideration in the decision to name someone to this strategic position. A centurion's tasks fell into two basic areas.

- *In combat*. The centurion was responsible for implementing military strategy. He would almost always be on point, leading the charge into battle.
- *Out of combat*. Away from the battlefield, the centurion administered discipline in the ranks, mediated interpersonal conflicts among his men, provided security and protection when called upon, supervised police actions in occupied areas, and, most notably for our purposes, would oversee executions. As a general rule, these executions were done by the sword for Roman citizens (Romans 13) and by crucifixion for all non-Romans.

Basically, a centurion was never off duty. This was the life of a career soldier, and combat involved a very unantiseptic approach to warfare. Unlike the surgical airstrikes and small-arms insertion teams so popular in today's military, the centurion's duty boiled down to one thing—the brutality of hand-to-hand combat. It was bloody and not at all glorious, but the battle went to the strongest and the most determined, and in those harsh conditions, a centurion learned how to be a survivor.

SOME CENTURIONS' EXPOSURE

As with all who crossed Christ's path (or that of His followers), centurions were greeted with concern, compassion, and the offer of love. There are six centurions mentioned in the New Testament, and several of these had significant roles. This significance is interesting because it shows the degree to which Christ's message and influence were crossing social, ethnic, and political lines and barriers. Notice several of the more prominent centurions in the New Testament and how Jesus and His apostles interacted with them:

- *The Centurion of Capernaum* (Matthew 8:5–13; Luke 7:1–10). This man came to Jesus on behalf of his servant. He exhibited both great submission (calling Jesus "Lord") and great faith in declaring that He believed that Christ need only say the word and the soldier's servant would be made whole. As if this weren't remarkable enough, the centurion of Capernaum gives us the unusual picture of the conquering warrior showing concern for a mere slave. To show such deep concern that he would seek out the Rabbi of Nazareth for help is truly amazing.

- *The Centurion of Caesarea (Acts 10:1, 22).* Cornelius, the first Gentile convert, was a centurion who had dealt kindly with and was appreciated by the Jewish people. Through his exposure to Judaism, his heart had been prepared for the seed of the gospel, and when Peter came to him with the message of the cross, he believed.

- *The Centurion of the Shipwreck (Acts 27–28).* Julius, the centurion responsible for delivering Paul to Rome for trial, was reluctant to accept the apostle's counsel at first. During the shipwreck experience, however, he was exposed to the vitality of Paul's faith and saw the power of God in the miraculous and saved Paul's life when it was threatened.

It is very important to notice something about these centurions. They were not the ancient equivalent of "the boy next door." They were the troops of an occupation force—professional soldiers that represented the iron heel of Rome and its subjugation and bondage. They represented everything that the Jews of the first century hated, yet, in spite of all that, one writer observed, "The centurions mentioned in the New Testament are uniformly spoken of in terms of praise, whether in the Gospels or in the Acts." Centurions were among the hated conquerors, brutal and swift in their approach to any and all problems—but always in the New Testament they are described in terms of respect.

That seems counterintuitive and is certainly unexpected. Perhaps these consistent descriptions are rooted in the evidence of their character. Roman historian Polybius noted a fact of great significance: Centurions were chosen by merit and were remarkable not so much for their daring courage and valor (although those qualities were important) as for their deliberation, constancy, and strength of mind. Bible scholar William Barclay quoted the ancient historian Polybius regarding centurions:

> They must not be so much venturesome seekers after danger as men who can command, steady in action and reliable; they ought not to be overanxious to rush into the fight, but when hard-pressed they must be ready to hold their ground and die at their posts.

Barclay, faced with this evidence, concluded, "The centurions were the finest men in the Roman army."

This historical background sets the stage for the centurion at the cross and the credibility of his words. His was not a statement from a frightened pup of a recruit or an easily manipulated conscript. It was the reasoned observation of a seasoned veteran who had watched men die—and had been putting them to their deaths—for his entire adult life. Centurions were required to be the models of steadiness and reserve. And all of that makes the faith of this one particular centurion all the more extraordinary.

ONE CENTURION'S FAITH

We hear the centurion of the cross make his great declaration in Matthew 27:54, where we read,

> Now the centurion, and those who were with him keeping guard over Jesus, when they saw the earthquake and the things that were happening, became very frightened and said, "Truly this was the Son of God."

Some have speculated about what the centurion meant—was it a confession of faith or a Roman trying to define something outside the scope of his experience? I believe, however, that the answer is in the context. Obviously the centurion was deeply moved by the events that he had witnessed, and the declaration of deity is what followed his observation. We need to consider two things in order to fully and carefully consider the magnitude of the centurion's words.

The evidence in opposition to the declaration. The evidence against such a declaration was strong indeed. This centurion could not ignore the strong condemnation of the Jewish religious leaders that had put Jesus on the cross for making the claim to be the Son of God. His commander-in-chief, Pontius Pilate, had upheld the conviction for Jesus' making that claim. Now the centurion rejects the condemnation and affirms Jesus' claim. Why? Because the evidence in favor of Christ's claim was overwhelming.

The evidence in support of the declaration. Remember, this man had no doubt been responsible for the supervision of many crucifixions. Yet there was something extraordinary, something remarkable, about this particular crucifixion that impacted the centurion in ways he could have never imagined when that day began. What did he see? There are several threads of evidence that combine to form a strong cord of truth.

- The *response* of Jesus to the injustice that He had been forced to endure at the hands of His own countrymen through arrest and trials.
- The *response* of Jesus to the torture that the centurion and his men had inflicted upon Him, recorded by Matthew:

   Then the soldiers of the governor took Jesus into the Praetorium and gathered the whole Roman cohort around Him. They stripped Him and put a scarlet robe on Him. And after twisting together a crown of thorns, they put it on His head, and a reed in His right hand; and they knelt down before Him and mocked Him, saying, "Hail, King of the Jews!" They spat on Him, and took the reed and began to beat Him on the head. After they had mocked Him, they took the scarlet robe off Him and put His own garments back on Him, and led Him away to crucify Him (Matthew 27:27–31).

- The *dignity* with which Jesus responded to the lynch mob that demanded His blood—as a sheep, silent before the slaughter.
- The **mercy** of Jesus toward the people who rejected Him and the soldiers that crucified Him—including this centurion. His response? "Father, forgive them!" even as they sat down to gamble (Matthew 27:35–36) for His meager possessions and to watch the gruesome spectacle (their only entertainment). Jesus' concern was for their forgiveness, not His own escape. That is powerful.
- Creation's *response* to the Creator's sin-bearing act. As Matthew records, witnesses "saw the earthquake and the things that were happening" (Matthew 27:54). They saw the sun go dark, they felt the power of the earth quaking under their feet—and they saw these supernatural phenomena suddenly end when Jesus yielded with a loud voice and died.

As a professional soldier who had no doubt supervised many executions and witnessed untold numbers of deaths, this centurion was understandably impressed by the significant events that accompanied the death of the Christ. In all of his vast and up-close exposure to death and dying, he had never seen such things before—and the impact on him was inescapable. As we read in the *Jamieson, Fausset, and Brown Bible Commentary*:

> There cannot be a reasonable doubt that this expression was used in the Jewish sense, and that it points to the claim which Jesus made to be the Son of God, and on which His condemnation expressly turned. The meaning, then, clearly is that He must have been what He professed to be; in other words, that He was no impostor. There was no medium between those two.

Herbert Lockyer adds, "What a remarkable testimony Christ received from this Gentile! How striking was the homage he paid to the crucified One at Golgotha!"

The centurion had seen it all, heard it all, and felt it all. As a result, he and his troops "became very frightened." Again, this was a group of battle-hardened soldiers with their centurion. They had experienced the terror of battle and had learned to cope with fear, but here they display sheer terror—not a true reverential fear, but, perhaps, as commentator John Gill wrote, the "fear of punishment: lest divine vengeance should light on them for their concern in this matter."

They had reason to be fearful because there was absolutely nothing ordinary about the significant events they were experiencing. It was:

- *No ordinary execution*. The darkness, the earthquake, and the cry of dereliction from Christ convinced the soldiers that this was no ordinary execution. The events terrified them and probably led them to believe that these things testified to heaven's wrath at the perpetration of such a crime, in which they themselves had participated. What great fear to suddenly realize you have put to death God's Son.

- *No ordinary power*. But there is more. They did not come to this conclusion at the announcement of some angelic messenger or apostolic preacher. Their conclusion came solely from the effects of the power of God on display at Calvary that dark day.

- *No ordinary confession*. This confession tells us something eternally important: Jesus as the promised Messiah and unique Son of God is seen most clearly in His passion and death. How interesting that the Jewish religious establishment had mocked Him with the title (vv. 41–44) by which a Roman centurion now confessed Him.

Matthew Henry wrote,

The dreadful appearances of God in His providence sometimes work strangely for the conviction and awakening of sinners. This was expressed in the terror that fell upon the centurion and the Roman soldiers. Let us, with an eye of faith, behold Christ and him crucified, and be affected with that great love wherewith he loved us. Never were the horrid nature and effects of sin so tremendously displayed, as on that day when the beloved Son of the Father hung upon the Cross, suffering for sin, the Just for the unjust, that He might bring us to God. Let us yield ourselves willingly to His service.

Church tradition has given the name Petronius to this centurion. If he was won to faith in Christ, he came as a pagan and, like the thief on the cross who believed, was saved as Jesus hung upon the cross. How simple and basic is that? All who are ever saved in truth are saved because of the death of Jesus on the cross. So the cross began to do its work at once. And that work has continued for two millennia, for the preaching of the cross may be foolishness to the world, but to those who are saved it is the power of God! No wonder Charles Wesley declared in his anthem of praise for the death of Christ, "Amazing love, how can it be, that Thou, my God, shouldst die for me!"

It was that powerful cross and the significance of the love displayed there that can change hearts—even the hardened, battle-weary heart of a career soldier—from death to life. The story is told of another soldier who also learned the significant lessons of Calvary. General Robert E. Lee, commander of the Confederate armies during America's Civil War, was attending a church service some time after the end of the war. At the conclusion of the sermon, Lee went forward to pray about things in his life that he had been convicted about during the message. As the great Confederate general knelt praying, a former slave likewise stepped forward and knelt beside him—praying for his own spiritual needs. Once he had finished praying, Lee rose to leave and was stopped by a Southern former slave-owner who bemoaned the fact that a black man would be allowed to kneel beside the great general. Lee, however, would have none of it, and responded. "The ground is always level at the foot of the cross."

It was in the first century, and it still is today. The foot of the cross is a place of significance where paupers and princes, religionists and pagans, well-knowns and unknowns, and—yes—generals and centurions find level ground to kneel and embrace the Christ who died for them—and for us.

THE WINDOW *of* SORROW

Joseph of Arimathea

As a pastor for over twenty years, I learned that there are many causes for joy and sorrow in ministry, but no cause for sorrow is as great as the heartache the bereaved feel at the death of a loved one. No deaths are easy to bear. All are a source of grief.

During many funerals, I have seen spouses or children or parents break down, weeping, and then turn to apologize for their tears. My response? Certainly no apology is necessary, but there is more to it than that. The vital nature of a relationship has been severed by death's angry scythe, leaving a tremendous depth of pain and loss, and this is all reflected in that tear-stained testimony. Whether mourners express their grief outwardly or bear it in silent sorrow, the reality is that grief is intense, and the intensity of grief is a reflection of the intensity of the love in the relationship between the bereaved and the deceased. Even though death evokes an intense emotional response, there are aspects of loss that can vary from situation to situation, so that every loss is colored by its own unique sorrow.

In some instances, a person's grief is deepened not just by a sense of loss but also by a feeling of loneliness that can be suffocating. This was certainly true of my mom when we lost my father to a heart attack in 1980. She grieved not just for the loss of a relationship but also for the loss of companionship after more than thirty years of marriage. As challenging as living life alone can be, it is all the more trying for the person who has lived life in a full and meaningful partnership and loses that partner to death.

There is something else, however. Grief can also be exacerbated by a heart of regret. A popular 1980's hit song, "In the Living Years," expresses the sorrow of lost relationship and lost opportunity that many people experience after a family member dies. In the crowning verse of the song, the singer's pain-ridden lyrics lament years of wasted struggle in a relationship with his father. He struggles with all that was left undone, finally remembering all those important things that had been left unsaid and wishing that he had been able to speak of those things with his dad "in the living years." Now his father is gone—and it is too late. The sorrow of regret is, indeed, a painful thing.

We could look to many people who knew and loved Christ and experienced a heavy burden of sorrow at His death, but we see a particularly touching portrait of true sorrow depicted by a man named Joseph—for he knew what it was not just to mourn, but to mourn from a heart of sorrow that may have been carrying the extra burden of regret.

According to *Strong's Exhaustive Concordance*, the name Joseph means "let him add," and it may reflect a desire and longing for prosperity. Like many of the Josephs of the Bible, Joseph of Arimathea was a noble character—but he also knew sorrow-filled regret.

A Man of Means

As we re-enter the story of our Lord's passion, the grisly task of crucifixion is now complete. The problem was that Jesus' body had to be cared for, and Judaism had strict guidelines on how that was and was not to occur—particularly on the eve of a Sabbath. It is at this point that Joseph enters the scene:

> When it was evening, there came a rich man from Arimathea, named Joseph, who himself had also become a disciple of Jesus (Matthew 27:57).

Matthew's record of Joseph's arrival is fascinating, for it reveals a number of things that, combined with the other gospel records, help to paint a surprising, even shocking, portrait of Joseph. While Matthew's statement is brief, Joseph's request was an event that would have shot thunderbolts through first-century Jerusalem. The prevailing assumption was that the followers of Christ were primarily poor, backwards Galileans with few redeeming qualities. Now, into the fray steps Joseph of Arimathea, and he certainly does not reflect the demographic profile. He is completely outside the stereotype in almost every way. Not only was he wealthy, he was not from Galilee. *Arimathea* means "heights" and "was the name of several cities in Palestine. The one mentioned in Matthew 27:57, Mark 15:43,

Luke 23:51, and John 19:38 appears to have been the same as the birthplace of Samuel in Mount Ephraim" (*Strong's Exhaustive Concordance*).

Not only did Joseph come from a different hometown from Jesus, he also bore a different social pedigree from the average follower of the Rabbi from Nazareth because he was wealthy. In any culture and language, rich means rich, and the person writing this account, Matthew, the former tax collector, knew a thing or two about money. For the Master who did not have any place to lay his head (Matthew 8:20) to have wealthy followers would have been quite surprising to the religious leaders who had plotted Jesus' death. In fact, respected commentator John Gill asserts that there are some who think that this man was Joseph ben Gurion, who may have been one of the richest priests in Jerusalem and a brother to Nicodemus, the Pharisee who secretly visited Jesus at night in John 3. One commentator speculated that Matthew's purpose in including this detail was intentional, for it would explain how Joseph would have access to Pilate and, as a result, the means not only to secure permission to bury the body but also to care for the preparation of the body and its ultimate burial. To be sure, Joseph of Arimathea was a man of social standing and means—someone to be reckoned with in Jerusalem's halls of power.

The most surprising piece of information about Joseph, however, is that he was a member of the Sanhedrin. Notice how Luke describes him:

> And a man named Joseph, who was a member of the Council, a good and righteous man (he had not consented to their plan and action), a man from Arimathea, a city of the Jews, who was waiting for the kingdom of God; this man went to Pilate and asked for the body of Jesus (Luke 23:50–52).

He was a member of the council that had condemned Jesus! He, along with Nicodemus, had no doubt resisted the kangaroo court's attempt to condemn the innocent Christ but had failed. Still, that Joseph and Nicodemus stood in that assembly and spoke against the course of action in defense of the Nazarene teacher must have shocked their fellow Sanhedrists. It is likely that in that moment of decision, any future Joseph had once anticipated as part of the favored ruling class was largely gone.

At this point, however, it seems that Joseph's once-valued wealth, which had seemed to carry so much clout and influence, was now useful only for caring for the crucified One.

A MAN OF FEAR

Stephen Crane's classic American work of fiction, *The Red Badge of Courage,* is set during America's Civil War, with young Henry Fleming as the lead character. In Crane's novel, we follow Fleming's irony-filled experiences as an eighteen-year-old soldier sent into battle. While the title of the book focuses on courage, irony comes from the reality that young Henry's heart is more characterized by fear. Driven by fear, Fleming deserts his battalion in the midst of battle—a choice he would come to regret deeply. His subsequent journey becomes one of shame and despair until he finally finds a kind of personal redemption. Henry ultimately goes into battle three times before finding the courage to conquer his fears.

That is how fear often works. Like Henry Fleming, we can be driven by our fears to do things that would otherwise be unthinkable, or fears can cause us to fail to do things that we know are right and good and necessary. When we allow fear to be the driving force behind our choices, the consequences can be devastating—a reality that is not limited to the genre of historical fiction. The theme of fear and its consequences occurs repeatedly in the pages of the Bible:

- It was fear that caused Adam to hide from God (Genesis 3:10).
- It was fear that caused Sarah to lie to God (Genesis 18:15).
- It was fear that caused Elijah to run and hide in a cave (1 Kings 19:3).
- It was fear that caused the parents of the man "born blind" to equivocate about their son's miraculous healing (John 9:22).
- It was fear that contributed to Pilate's decision to crucify Jesus (John 19:8).

Without question, fear can be a truly crippling emotion. Fear can become a force that enslaves our hearts, resulting in the pain of regret—leaving us haunted by the "what ifs," "if onlys," and "I should'ves" that come as we second-guess our own shortcomings. Henry Fleming felt it. I have felt it. Perhaps you have felt it. And, I would suggest, Joseph of Arimathea felt it. And, if so, his regrets were the fruit of what he had failed to do because of fear. In John's account of the events of Calvary we read:

> After these things Joseph of Arimathea, being a disciple of Jesus, but a secret one for fear of the Jews..." (19:38).

"A secret one." Out of fear, Joseph had not publicly identified with Christ. Now he had the regret of knowing his life was less than it might have been if he had boldly set his course with the Messiah. Fear can be a terrible thing—an unforgiving thing. And the Scriptures have much to tell us about it. Sometimes, the word *fear* refers to a healthy, holy reverence for the God of heaven. But not here. Joseph's fear was of men and their retaliation or mockery or even worse—their persecution. Joseph's fear was directly opposed to the challenge of the Savior himself when He said, "I say to you, My friends, do not be afraid of those who kill the body and after that have no more that they can do" (Luke 12:4). But Joseph *had* feared—choosing the contradictory path of "secret discipleship."

What are you afraid of? As I write this, I am sitting in an airport lounge that is normally overflowing with passengers traveling the world. But "normally" was before the economic crash, and this airport is empty. Where there was once the buzz of commerce and economic energy, now there is fear. In today's uncertain climate, some fear the loss of their jobs. Others the loss of their pensions. Others the loss of their status as leaders in a business community that seems to lack leadership.

What are you afraid of? I just spoke with a friend who is recovering from cancer—always knowing that what is now in remission could return tomorrow. A colleague and his wife have seen their worst fears come true as they have, in recent days, buried their preschool-age son who was taken by cancer. Another parent I know fears that with the current economic troubles, he will be unable to care for the health of his children if they *do* become ill.

What are you afraid of? Joseph was afraid of people— and sometimes we are as well. Afraid of wagging tongues and mean-spirited looks. Afraid of standing up and raising our hand and declaring of Christ, "I am His and He is mine."

For all of us, as we wrestle with fear, the Bible tells us some things that we need to read and reread and read yet again:

- For God hath not given us the spirit of fear; but of power, and of love, and of a sound mind (2 Timothy 1:7 KJV).

- So that we may boldly say, "The Lord is my helper, and I will not fear what man shall do unto me" (Hebrews 13:6 KJV).
- There is no fear in love; but perfect love casts out fear, because fear involves punishment, and the one who fears is not perfected in love (1 John 4:18).

Perhaps that is why one of our Lord's favorite reminders to His men was, "Fear not." The paralyzing nature of fear will destroy us unless we surrender it to the perfect love of the One who can cast out our fears. Only there, in His perfect care, can we know peace. So He reminds us to "fear not."

But Joseph *had* feared, and with his Messiah condemned and crucified, he carried that extra burden with his grief. He had been driven by fear rather than faith, and with His Lord's death on the cross, he bore the weight of his failings. He had succumbed to the fear of men, and this fear had led him to choose the safety of secret discipleship.

It is critical, however, that we see that this was not something that Joseph could never recover from. Joseph's life of fear may have resulted in a battle with regrets, but his love for the Savior finally drove out those fears. Joseph, the once fearful, became Joseph the determined. First, he demonstrated courage during Jesus' trial when he did not consent to the Savior's death (Luke 23:50). Then, he boldly stood before the Roman procurator who had ordered Jesus' execution and identified with the crucified One. I like the way the New American Standard Bible puts it:

Joseph of Arimathea came, a prominent member of the Council, who himself was waiting for the kingdom of God; and he gathered up courage and went in before Pilate, and asked for the body of Jesus (Mark 15:43).

This man of fear "gathered up courage" and confronted Pilate—despite his own involvement in the Council that ruled in favor of the death of the Savior—and requested permission to care for Jesus' body. It was an act of daring from a heart perhaps more accustomed to fear, but perhaps it revealed a fresh determination. Once, Joseph had failed to take a stand for Christ, but no more. Now Joseph identified with the condemned Christ (something that, in itself, would have been extremely dangerous) and asked the most powerful man in the nation to allot the care of the body to him. Somewhat surprisingly, Pilate, who could have had Joseph arrested for being an associate of the executed Rabbi, released the body of Jesus to him.

A MAN WHO CARED

In the movie version of the television show *The Fugitive,* Richard Kimble (having been found guilty of murdering his wife and sentenced to death) has escaped custody and is being pursued by federal marshal Lt. Sam Gerard. After a relentless hunt, Gerard finally has his quarry trapped in a drain overlooking a tall dam. With his hands raised in surrender, Kimble declares to his pursuer, "I didn't kill my wife!" To that desperate plea, Gerard replies, "Richard, I don't care!" In shock, Kimble seeks to flee for his life rather than surrender to the authorities.

Sometimes the world feels exactly like that exchange. We cry out the deepest pain of our hearts, and the world responds, "I don't care." This is nothing new. David, like Richard Kimble, was hunted down like an animal and wrote while hiding in a cave, "Look to the right and see; for there is no one who regards me; there is no escape for me; no one cares for my soul" (Psalm 142:4). That probably comes close to summing up how Richard Kimble felt as well.

It is a harsh world, where caring for others is most often seen as an unnecessary risk at best and absolute foolishness at worst. And that's caring for "others" who are still alive. But why take the risk to care about those who are dead? Perhaps it is the coldness of that logic that shows us that there is something noble and honorable about wanting to show proper care and respect for those who have left this life. In *The Parable of Joy*, his commentary on the gospel of John, Michael Card points to the sacrificial nature of Joseph and Nicodemus' care for Jesus' body, noting that the last thing they would have wanted to do, as high-ranking Pharisees, would be to touch a dead body and be rendered unclean for Passover. This willingness to go to the utmost to care for the body of Jesus shows the extent of Joseph's caring.

I was sitting on a plane, waiting for boarding to be completed for a short flight. As folks continued to board, the pilot came on the PA system and asked the folks on the right side of the plane to lower their window shades. Why? "One of our young soldiers has just returned from Iraq, and we need to give the family privacy as they welcome him home." I turned to lower my shade, and, on the tarmac, I saw a flag-draped coffin being loaded into a hearse with a weeping, grief-stricken group of family and friends watching.

The pilot's gesture of care and concern was not extraordinary—and maybe that is why it had so much impact. For the next few minutes, you could hear the soft sounds of people crying throughout the plane—sharing in the grief of the family of a dead soldier. It was a show of respect and appreciation for the sacrifice of one taken by death. The passengers' reaction was touching in its simplicity and sincerity, and it reminded me that sometimes we human beings have great capacity for kindness—in spite of ourselves.

In the midst of this harsh world that so often does *not* care, Joseph of Arimathea, who had previously been too afraid to publicly identify with Christ when the Savior was alive, now does the unthinkable and identifies with Him in His death. It might have seemed odd to Pilate that someone would claim this "criminal's" body, because history tells us that usually the Romans' final humiliation for the victim of a crucifixion was leaving the dead body for beasts of prey, denying the deceased a proper burial. John's record shows us how the once-fearful Joseph's expression of care contrasts with this Roman custom as he lavishes burial preparations on the body of Jesus.

> After these things Joseph of Arimathea, being a disciple of Jesus, but a secret one for fear of the Jews, asked Pilate that he might take away the body of Jesus; and Pilate granted permission. So he came and took away His body. Nicodemus, who had first come to Him by night, also came, bringing a mixture of myrrh and aloes, about a hundred pounds weight. So they took the body of Jesus and bound it in linen wrappings with the spices, as is the burial custom of the Jews. Now in the place where He was crucified there was a garden, and in the garden a new tomb in which no one had yet been laid. Therefore because of the Jewish day of preparation, since the tomb was nearby, they laid Jesus there (John 19:38–42).

Just the physical struggle of removing the battered and bloody body of the Savior from the cross would have been a challenging task—and a gruesome one. The body would then have to be transported to the tomb where it would be prepared for burial in that "new" tomb John described. The burial site was not selected randomly, however. That new tomb was Joseph's own tomb (Matthew 27:60). The tomb would be one last gift—one final expression of love from

Joseph of Arimathea to the crucified Christ. There, in a garden of beauty, Joseph and a few of Jesus' disciples performed a task both horrible and lovely. They prepared the body of Jesus for burial with care and attention to detail, all the while aware that time was running out—they must be finished before the start of the Sabbath.

In *The Life and Times of Jesus the Messiah*, Alfred Edersheim describes the burial scene and all its sad, solemn dignity:

> It was in 'the court' of the tomb that the hasty embalmment—if such it may be called—took place. None of Christ's former disciples seem to have taken part in the burying... Only a few faithful ones, notably among them Mary Magdalene and the other Mary, the mother of Joses, stood over against the tomb, watching at some distance where and how the Body of Jesus was laid... From where they stood they could only have had a dim view of what passed within the court, and this may explain how, on their return, they 'prepared spices and ointments' for the more full honours which they hoped to pay the Dead after the Sabbath was past. For, it is of the greatest importance to remember, that haste characterised all that was done. It seems as if the 'clean linen cloth' in which the Body had been wrapped, was now torn into 'cloths' or swathes, into which the Body, limb by limb, was now 'bound,' no

doubt, between layers of myrrh and aloes, the Head being wrapped in a napkin. And so they laid Him to rest in the niche of the rock-hewn new tomb. And as they went out, they rolled, as was the custom, a 'great stone'—the *Golel*—to close the entrance to the tomb...

The Christ whose death had caused the veil of the temple to rip apart from top to bottom was now being buried in the torn linen burial cloths that were lovingly applied by Joseph and Nicodemus—two men in religious fellowship who had confronted the justice system to secure the body of the innocent One. Two men whose secret fears gave way to a very public demonstration of love, devotion, and care. And perhaps both Joseph and Nicodemus bore the sorrow of regret about what, humanly speaking, might have been, had they declared their allegiance to the Savior sooner. Now it was too late for regret—but it was not too late to care.

How did the story end for Joseph? His faith and his perspective on the sufferings of Christ through the window of sorrow are clearly depicted in the Gospels, but there is no mention of his future outcome. I've been fascinated by questions about what happened to Joseph of Arimathea after the burial of Jesus ever since I read Donna Fletcher Crow's intriguing work of historical fiction *Glastonbury*, an account she bases on the legends of ancient church tradition. Tradition says that Joseph of Arimathea, with his family and some friends, became missionaries to ancient England. According to a legend that first appears in William of Malmesbury, Philip sent Joseph to Britain in AD 63, where he founded the first Christian settlement, which came to be known as Glastonbury. A later legend, from around 1200, claims that Joseph brought the Holy Grail to England.

Is the story true? We won't know until we are with Joseph in the presence of Christ, but if it is, it means that Joseph of Arimathea's public display of devotion for Christ was not limited to providing a proper burial for the Rabbi. It means that he overcame his fear, and his sorrow may have dissipated as he reached a new land with the message of the once-buried, now risen Savior. It means that his regrets were replaced with active commitment that advanced the gospel. It means that Joseph's failure as a disciple was supplanted by his perseverance as a missionary. It means that sorrow over Christ's death gave way to the joy of telling others the message of everlasting life.

As for me, I really do hope it is true.

THE WINDOW of STRENGTH

The Women

There is a physical reality that, in general, men are stronger than women. It is why you don't see women playing professional football at the same competitive level as men. It is why, even at the professional level, women golfers play from tees that are closer to the hole than the tees for their male counterparts. In general, that men tend to be physically stronger than women is something almost universally agreed upon.

This physical reality, however, should not be extrapolated into a position or perspective that would view women as in any way inferior to men. Nor, in particular, should the idea that men tend to be stronger than women lead us to conclude that women are weak (remember, the Bible refers to women as a weaker vessel, but not a weak one [1 Peter 3:7]). Such a conclusion is the worst kind of foolishness. The examples of strong women in the pages of history are legion—and deserve to be taken seriously. Acknowledging the physical strength of men should in no way cause us to negate the strength that women have displayed and do display—not only physically, but in every arena of life. For example, consider these women who showed great strength in a variety of ways.

- The strength of courage that pioneer airplane pilot Amelia Earhart displayed, seen in her fearless determination to accomplish the kinds of feats that in her generation were usually the singular domain of men and making her one of the most distinguished, courageous pilots of her day.

- Madame Curie's strength of intellect. She was the only person to win Nobel prizes in two different sciences—physics and chemistry—making her one of the leading scientists of her generation. Her work in the field of radiation was groundbreaking and continues to impact our lives in many ways today.

- The physical strength of Babe Didrikson Zaharias made her one of the greatest athletes of all time. Multitalented, Zaharias was able to excel in golf, track and field, and basketball—even competing against men in a number of PGA tour events. In the events she played against men, she missed the cut only once—in her first event.

- Golda Meir's strength of perseverance made her a leader who rose to the position of prime minister of Israel. She was able, against all odds, to lead the young nation through one of the most trying seasons in its history—the famous Yom Kippur War of 1973. The first Israeli prime minster, David Ben-Gurion, used to call Meir "the best man in the government" despite the public characterization of her as a kindly, but strong-willed, Jewish grandmother.

These were women who had the strength to stand among men as equals and even to surpass them in many ways. Yet these instances are not as isolated as they may seem. In our generation, we see the strength of women in all walks of life. To somehow suppose that women are weak is to miss the point.

You might be asking, "Okay, what's the point? Aren't we making 'much ado about nothing' here?" To the contrary, I believe that this is necessary background for us to have as we look at the passion of Christ through the next window of experience—the window of strength. For it was primarily the women—not the men—who displayed the strength of devotion and commitment to walk with Him through His final dark hours. With the exception of John, it was not the disciples at the foot of Christ's cross. It was the women. It was not the disciples attending to the burial of the Master, it was Nicodemus and Joseph of Arimathea—with the women there the entire time. It was not the disciples who, out of passion and desire to have a final time of ministry and service to the crucified Lord, made their way to the tomb that first resurrection day. It was the women.

They displayed a level of strength that the other followers of Christ did not. Why? Rather than make excuses for the men, I think we need instead to see and honor the strength in the hearts of the women. Seeing the events from the perspective of their hearts will illuminate the suffering of the Savior in a way that no spotlight ever could. Their strength opens a window that allows us to see things we might have otherwise missed.

THE STRENGTH OF DEVOTION

If we are to appreciate the level of strength exhibited by the women at the cross and the tomb, we need to move backwards in time to the earlier days of Jesus' public ministry, and we need to understand the times in which Jesus lived.

In the time of Christ, women were not highly prized. In fact, the normal Jewish religious scholar would, as a practice, pray with thanksgiving to God that he had not been made a Gentile, a Samaritan, or a woman. Men had the strength of power, and women were largely dominated by the men of ancient culture and were considered possessions of their husbands, with no legal rights and no opportunities for education. So undervalued were women in the ancient world that it was not unusual for female infants to be cast on the trash heap to be allowed to die rather than to be another mouth to feed. To put it mildly, the ancient world was not a place concerned with gender equity or anything even remotely approaching it.

Then Jesus came. Jesus, revealed with great care and clarity in Luke's gospel record, showed respect for women that was uncommon in first-century Israel. He treated women with honor and dignity, with kindness and care. He was continually violating the social taboos of His generation, breaking down barriers of prejudice and discrimination, and made women welcome members of His kingdom.

In a day when religious training was restricted to men, Jesus taught women the principles of the kingdom. In a day when justice was reserved for the protection of male rights, He intervened to protect those without the political or cultural clout to protect themselves. In a day when men were supposed to rule and women were supposed to be used, He honored the sacrifices of worship made by women—even though the men thought those acts scandalous. Everything was different because Jesus came.

In that day, it should not be surprising, then, that strong women of devotion and faith were drawn to Christ and numbered prominently among His followers. Notice Luke's account of some of those women:

> Soon afterwards, He began going around from one city and village to another, proclaiming and preaching the kingdom of God. The twelve were with Him, and also some women who had been healed of evil spirits and sicknesses: Mary who was called Magdalene, from whom seven demons had gone out, and Joanna the wife of Chuza, Herod's steward, and Susanna, and many others who were contributing to their support out of their private means (Luke 8:1–3).

Again, this is remarkable because it was so radically countercultural for that day. Rabbis taught *men*. Rabbis had *male* disciples. Christ's intentional inclusion of women was extraordinary. Who were the women numbered here among the followers of Christ?

Mary of Magdala

She is often portrayed in literature and film as a prostitute, but there is no biblical evidence to support that supposition. What we *do* know is that Mary was demon possessed, and Jesus rescued her from that demonization (Luke 8:2). Of all the characters delivered from demons by Christ in the Gospels, none showed such consistent devotion to the Savior as this Mary. And she is present both throughout Christ's anguish and at the discovery of the empty tomb. Those who speculate about her moral character would be better served by studying her passion and devotion to the One who set her free. We can learn much from her commitment to the Savior.

Joanna

Joanna was the wife of Chuza, the steward of Herod Antipas, who was tetrarch of Galilee (Luke 8:3). She was one of the women who ministered to our Lord and to whom He appeared after His resurrection (Luke 8:3; 24:10). But that doesn't really drive home the point. The key, I think, is that she was married to Chuza, who was the primary household servant of Herod Antipas. It was this Herod who had executed John the Baptizer and who, with his men, humiliated Christ after Pilate had found no fault with Him.

Chuza must have been greatly conflicted—relieved that the power of Christ had transformed his wife, yet fearful of the political danger of being seen as a Christ sympathizer. One commentary explains, "That [Chuza] was a disciple of Christ is very improbable, though he might be favorably disposed towards Him. But what we know not of him, and may fear he lacked, we are sure his wife possessed. Healed either of 'evil spirits' or of some one of the 'infirmities' here referred to—the ordinary diseases of humanity—she joins in the Saviour's train of grateful, clinging followers." If Joanna's allegiance to Christ with its potential for political problems bothered Chuza, it did not stop her from faithfully following Christ all the way to the tomb.

Susanna

Susanna, which means "lily," is the least known of these women, but we clearly see her commitment as she supports the mission and work of Christ and His disciples along with these other devoted women.

Notice that Luke also informs us (8:3) that there were "many others who were contributing to their support out of their private means." These women were committed to following Christ—and they showed the extent of their commitment by their financial support. There is strength in that devotion, particularly in a day when women's participation in religious activities was frowned upon. These women weren't just interested bystanders—they were devoted followers.

But the journey does not end here for the spiritually strong women who followed Jesus. We find them next at the foot of the cross.

THE STRENGTH OF COURAGE

Therefore the soldiers did these things. But standing by the cross of Jesus were His mother, and His mother's sister, Mary the wife of Clopas, and Mary Magdalene (John 19:25).

"But standing by the cross of Jesus..." John puts the scene into focus by reporting both who is there, and who is not. We do not see Peter, the brash, outspoken fisherman-disciple. We do not see Andrew, his brother. We do not see James or Simeon or any of the other chosen followers of Jesus. It was just too dangerous to be identified with a condemned criminal. Such recklessness could land you on the next cross to be erected on that skull-like hill. But the women are there—despite the danger. William Barclay wrote of these women who faithfully and courageously followed Jesus:

> Some say that because women were so unimportant in that culture, that no one would really notice their presence—and they ran no risk in being there. In fact, it was always a dangerous thing to be an

associate of a man considered so dangerous by the Roman government that he deserved a cross. It is always a dangerous thing to demonstrate one's love for someone the orthodox regard as a heretic. The presence of these women at the cross was not due to the fact that they were so unimportant that no one would notice them—their presence was due to the fact that perfect love casts out fear.

Who were they? Gathered on Golgotha to watch the Savior die was an unusual mix of women with distinct personalities and a variety of life experiences. In addition to Mary Magdalene and the other women already mentioned, there were several more in this group of Christ-followers.

Mary, the Mother of Jesus

That moment that Jesus hung on the cross became the agonizing fulfillment of words that had been spoken to Mary three decades earlier. After the birth of Jesus, when she and Joseph had brought the child to the temple, an aged man, Simeon, stepped into the temple and declared the arrival of Messiah. His words of joy were muted, however, by the words of prophecy he spoke to Mary. We read in Luke 2:34–35:

> Behold, this Child is appointed for the fall and rise of many in Israel, and for a sign to be opposed—and a sword will pierce even your own soul—to the end that thoughts from many hearts may be revealed.

Tucked away in those words of victory and joy was that phrase pregnant with pain, "and a sword will pierce even your own soul." Now, the agony of watching her Son die becomes that sword of grief and suffering that Mary had feared for so many years.

Salome, the Rebuked (Mary's Sister)

In John she is not named, but from the parallel passages (Mark 15:40; Matthew 27:56) it becomes clear that she is Salome, the mother of James and John (making them cousins of Jesus). The interesting thing about her presence at the cross was that she had received a stern rebuke from Jesus in Matthew 20:20–23 when she had sought the chief places in the kingdom for her sons. Though she had been rebuked, her presence at the cross says much for her and for Christ. It shows that she had the humility to accept the rebuke and to love on with undiminished devotion. It also showed that Jesus was able to rebuke in such a way that His love was still evident.

Mary, the Wife of Cleopas

Commentary writer and theologian Adam Clarke pointed out that Mary, the wife of Cleopas was the mother of James the Less and Joses (Matthew 27:56; Mark 15:40). Matthew 10:3 tells us that this James was the son of Alpheus, and so it appears that Alpheus and Cleopas must have been the same person. It is added, in some ancient histories, that

Cleopas was the brother of Joseph, the husband of Mary. Biblical scholar John Gill added, "This Mary was no doubt a believer in Christ, and came and stood by his cross; not merely to keep her sister company, but out of affection to Jesus, and to testify her faith in him."

Most of the Christ-followers that we see gathered at the foot of the cross were women. As Jesus had warned, the disciples (aside from John) were unprepared for the horrors of this day and were in hiding—including Peter, whose great boasts of staying with Jesus even to the death now had a sad and hollow ring. It was the women who, at no small amount of personal risk, continued to identify themselves with the Master, even as He died for them. It was the women who stood there, no doubt feeling the anger and abuse of the crowd. It was the women who showed the strength of courage simply to be there.

In addition, Gill sees this important application in the women's presence at the cross: "[It] may teach us to do as they did, look upon the crucified Christ, view His sorrows, and His sufferings, and our sins laid upon Him, and taken away by Him. We should look unto him for pardon, cleansing, and justification, and, in short, for the whole of salvation. We should also weep, as they did, whilst we look on him; shed even tears of affection for, and sympathy with him; of humiliation for sin, and of joy for a Savior: and likewise should abide by him as they did, by his persons, offices, and grace; by the doctrine of the cross, continuing steadfastly in it, and that notwithstanding all reproaches and sufferings we may undergo." Courage that stands alone, however, could be nothing more than reckless bravado. Their courage was more—it was fueled by their love.

THE STRENGTH OF LOVE

Greek scholar and Bible teacher A. T. Robertson wrote, "We have come to expect the women from Galilee to be faithful, last at the Cross and first at the tomb." And they were. Our look through the window of sorrow of Joseph of Arimathea showed us that the women who were at the cross had followed Joseph to the burial site, and they saw the tomb and the burial preparations. Luke tells us about what the women did at the tomb:

> Now the women who had come with Him out of Galilee followed, and saw the tomb and how His body was laid. Then they returned and prepared spices and perfumes. And on the Sabbath they rested according to the commandment (Luke 23:55–56).

Following the Sabbath rest, however, these women who had followed Jesus in Galilee and then followed Him from there now made what must have felt like one final trek in service of the Master. They went to the tomb to complete the burial process that had been cut short by the arrival of Shabbat:

> But on the first day of the week, at early dawn, they came to the tomb bringing the spices which they had prepared (Luke 24:1).

The hurried burial process that had begun on crucifixion day needed to be completed, and the women had worked to prepare for that sad and somber task. Interestingly, each of the Gospels records the presence of women at the tomb that first Lord's Day morning. While none seem to contain the entire list of those attending to Christ's burial, each gospel writer focuses on the part of the story he wants us to see.

- Matthew mentions Mary Magdalene and the "other Mary" (apparently, the wife of Cleopas and mother of James)
- Mark mentions Mary Magdalene, Mary the mother of James, and Salome
- John focuses his account on the interactions between Jesus and Mary Magdalene.
- Luke's record (the gospel account that most clearly shows Jesus' countercultural care and respect for women) seems to be the most comprehensive: "Now they were Mary Magdalene and Joanna and Mary the mother of James; also the other women with them were telling these things to the apostles" (Luke 24:10).

In Luke's record we see them—brokenhearted but still devoted, grieving but still engaged, overwhelmed but still serving. Mark tells us that as they approached the tomb, they wondered how they might remove the grave stone so that they could minister to the body of Jesus. But as it turned out, that would not be a concern. Again, in Luke, we see the familiar words that we hear every Easter Sunday— words so familiar we may have lost the majesty of what we see. Words stated in such a matter-of-fact way that we may not fully appreciate the emotional impact of the events described here.

> And they found the stone rolled away from the tomb, but when they entered, they did not find the body of the Lord Jesus. While they were perplexed about this, behold, two men suddenly stood near them in dazzling clothing; and as the women were terrified and bowed their faces to the ground, the men said to them, "Why do you seek the living One among the dead? He is not here, but He has risen. Remember how He spoke to you while He was still in Galilee, saying that the Son of Man must be delivered into the hands of sinful men, and be crucified, and the third day rise again." And they remembered His words, and returned from the tomb and reported all these things to the eleven and to all the rest. Now they were Mary Magdalene and Joanna and Mary the mother of James; also the other women

with them were telling these things to the apostles
(Luke 24:2–10).

In their grief-stricken despair, they arrived at the tomb
to encounter the one thing they had never anticipated—the
tomb was empty. John's gospel tells of the personal sense of
loss and devastation Mary Magdalene felt at the discovery
of the body's disappearance. It was not just that the tomb
was empty—Mary, who had such a deep sense of love and
indebtedness to the Christ for His powerful rescue of her
heart and life, felt doubly robbed. She was not only robbed
of the body of the Master, she was also robbed of one final,
tragic opportunity to serve the Rabbi of Galilee. But the
emotional impact of the empty tomb reached further than
Mary's broken heart.

The women of Galilee would experience an emotional
roller coaster of feelings that is hard to appreciate as we
read the story two millennia later. Luke tells us that the
women (Luke 24:4) were "perplexed," which in the Greek
means "to be entirely at loss." The word conveys utter confusion, explaining what was *not* there, the body of Jesus. This
perplexity, however, turned to terror (v. 5) and amazement
(Mark 16:5) when they saw who *was* there—the angelic
messengers of resurrection day who sent them to the fearful disciples in hiding with word that the Savior was alive!
Upon hearing the message of the resurrected Christ, they
fled from the tomb, because "trembling and astonishment
had gripped them" (Mark 16:8). But as the import of what

they had seen and heard in the cemetery took hold, the emotional landscape shifted once again—as "they left the tomb quickly with fear and great joy" (Matthew 28:8).

The strength of their love had caused them to follow Jesus in the Galilee and to follow Him to Jerusalem and to stand by Him at the cross and to follow again to His burial and, ultimately, make this final, fateful mission of mercy to the Master who had rescued them from the demons of darkness and the oppressions of indignity. God was rewarding the strong devotion, courage, and love that motivated them to follow. As Hebrews 6:10 tells us:

> For God is not unjust so as to forget your work and the love which you have shown toward His name, in having ministered and in still ministering to the saints.

If the heavenly Father remembers the acts of love and kindness done in His name to others, how much more the selfless acts of love these women had ministered to His Son? Matthew tells us that as they were making their way to the place where the disciples were in hiding, the greatest moment of joy they would ever know occurred. The message the angels had delivered at the tomb was confirmed— by the physical appearance of Christ himself!

> And they left the tomb quickly with fear and great joy and ran to report it to His disciples. And behold, Jesus met them and greeted them. And they came

up and took hold of His feet and worshiped Him. Then Jesus said to them, "Do not be afraid; go and take word to My brethren to leave for Galilee, and there they will see Me" (Matthew 28:8–10).

Love that had sought no reward had nevertheless been rewarded. The fear and confusion is taken from their heart by His gift of peace and grace. These women of Galilee had suffered much but now knew the matchless privilege of being the first in many marvelous, overwhelming, grace-filled firsts:

> The first at the cross
> The first at the tomb
> The first to hear of the resurrection
> The first to see the risen, glorious Son of God
> The first to tell the story of the Prince of
> Life's defeat of death

Through the window of these women, we see clearly that the only appropriate response is to do what they did: worship the Christ and tell others of His victory. It is an event that demands we bow the knee to the risen Lord and share the joy with a dying world. As another incredibly strong woman, Fanny Crosby, put it in her marvelous hymn "Christ Is Risen":

> Christ hath risen! Hallelujah!
> Friends of Jesus, dry your tears;

Through the veil of gloom and darkness,
Lo, the Son of God appears!
Christ is risen! Hallelujah!
Gladness fills the world today;
From the tomb that could not hold Him,
See, the stone is rolled away!

We see strength on display in the lives of these godly women. It is my desire that their example would stir my heart—and yours—to rise to a new strength of devotion, of courage, and of love for the Son of God who loved us and gave himself for us (Galatians 2:20). To "be strong in the Lord and in the strength of His might" (Ephesians 6:10). Or, as the psalmist put it:

> Be strong and let your heart take courage,
> All you who hope in the LORD (Psalm 31:24).

THE WINDOW *of* SCRIPTURE

The Emmaus Road Travelers

grew up going to church. Mine was not an atypical experience at the church I attended in West Virginia. I remember the flannelgraph stories of Bible heroes from days gone by. I remember sitting in the balcony and watching the services unfold. I remember being impressed by the liturgy and even occasionally being moved by the music. But something seemed to be missing. There was an abundance of religious vocabulary and loads of activity and even a certain level of commitment. But something was missing. There were stained glass windows and choir robes and a pulpit and an organ. But something was missing.

Now understand that, in and of themselves, none of those things are wrong or evil or sinful. On the contrary, in their place they can be wonderful—even inspirational. But something was missing. As a boy, I couldn't begin to understand what that missing element might be. There was a hollowness to it all, and even though at that age I had not yet heard Shakespeare's words, let alone grasped their meaning, my church experience seemed to be "full of sound and fury, signifying nothing."

Then, as a young adult, I was invited to visit a church that had almost all those same elements—but with a difference. Slowly, surely, ultimately, it became clear. What church #2 had that church #1 lacked came into focus: the power of the Word of God. Don't get me wrong—church #1 had sermons. But it lacked the power of the Word of God. Compelled by that extraordinary powerful Word, I came to

Christ as my Savior and Lord, and while I have often failed Him, I have continued to see remarkable expressions of the abiding power of the Scriptures.

- I have seen the power of the Word of God to comfort a grieving mother suffering the death of her child.
- I have seen the power of the Word of God to restore relationships that were not merely broken—they were shattered, seemingly beyond repair.
- I have seen the power of the Word of God to cross cultural barriers and reach into the hearts of people so diverse that they make the United Nations look monochromatic.
- I have seen the power of the Word of God to take people of absolutely profligate, degenerate lives (like mine) and redeem them through the work of Christ.

It is an extraordinary thing, really, that God, who spoke the world into existence (by the power of His word) and revealed himself to us most clearly through the Logos— the living Word, Jesus, who became flesh and dwelt among us to rescue us from our sins—has likewise spoken to us through His written word, the Bible. And powerful it is—as the writer of Hebrews asserts in familiar words:

> For the word of God is living and powerful, and sharper than any two-edged sword, piercing even to the division of soul and spirit, and of joints and

marrow, and is a discerner of the thoughts and intents of the heart (Hebrews 4:12 NKJV).

And, because of that, it is of inestimable significance that, at the end of the first resurrection day, it would be that living, powerful Word of God that would bring comfort, insight, and help to followers of Jesus trying to unravel the shocking events of the passion of the Christ.

QUESTIONS AND CONFUSION

The first time I traveled outside of North America was, to say the least, a stretching experience. First, the travel was like nothing I had ever encountered—foreign airports with foreign languages, foreign people, foreign smells, and foreign foods. It was so strange that it took some time before I realized that it wasn't everything else that was foreign—*I* was the foreigner.

Making my way from gate to gate at Schiphol Airport in Amsterdam was one of the more unsettling episodes of my life. Nothing made sense. I didn't know what I was supposed to do or how I was supposed to do it. I didn't know where I was supposed to go or how I was supposed to get there. My mind was filled with questions, but I had no one to ask. It was much more than unsettling—it was disorienting. The first two weeks of that trip, I felt like I was in an emotional blender, being constantly turned and churned and kept off balance by things I didn't understand and couldn't properly process. I was in a different world—a world the Temptations of the 1960s sang about as a "Ball of Confusion."

That is what confusion does to us—it raises questions that seem to have no answers and creates a deeply disturbing sense of mental and emotional vertigo to which we simply do not know how to respond. It's tough. And this condition can even get worse because, without answers to our questions and clarity for our confusion, we feel as if we are sinking deeper and deeper into the fog of "not knowing."

It is in just such a fog that we join the characters of the passion story in Luke 24. Here, we find two Christ-followers on the first Sunday after the crucifixion. All that they thought they knew and believed had been swept away in a whirlwind of events that had left their Messiah dead and their faith shattered. Or so they thought. But the power of the Word of God, spoken to them by the Son of God, would lift the fog of their confusion and give a new and fresh clarity to their purpose for living.

The Presence of the Christ (vv. 13–16)

And behold, two of them were going that very day to a village named Emmaus, which was about seven miles from Jerusalem. And they were talking with each other about all these things which had taken place. While they were talking and discussing, Jesus Himself approached and began traveling with them. But their eyes were prevented from recognizing Him.

It is fascinating to me that, after the resurrection, Jesus had a physical presence—but it was unlike ours, creating a challenging framework for the experiences His followers had with Him in the days of His resurrection. They simply had no reference point for what they would see in Him. Earlier that morning, Mary Magdalene (John 20:15) had failed to recognize Christ in the garden. Then, in the evening, when Jesus appeared to His disciples, He suddenly just "stood in their midst" (Luke 24:36) while they were in hiding behind locked doors. And yet, while He was capable of appearing and disappearing, of coming and going even through locked doors and stone walls, He also expressed a desire to eat some broiled fish and honeycomb (Luke 24:42), just as a person with an ordinary physical body. The physician Luke, a man whose medical training would give him special interest in such things, notably provides details on the resurrected body of Jesus.

Once again, the extraordinary nature of His resurrected form is in view here, on the road to Emmaus. Jesus appears to two of His followers, but for reasons unstated they are "prevented from recognizing Him" (v. 16).

The Heartaches of the Moment (vv. 17–20)

And He said to them, "What are these words that you are exchanging with one another as you are walking?" And they stood still, looking sad. One of them, named Cleopas, answered and said to Him, "Are You the only one visiting Jerusalem and unaware of the things which have happened here in these days?" And He said to them, "What things?" And they said to Him, "The things about Jesus the Nazarene, who was a prophet mighty in deed and word in the sight of God and all the people, and how the chief priests and our rulers delivered Him to the sentence of death, and crucified Him.

As Jesus joined these men in their walk, He immediately began to probe their wounded hearts. What I find interesting here is that one of these men is identified as Cleopas (v. 18), undoubtedly the same Cleopas whose wife, Mary, was among the women who had brought the word back to the distraught disciples that the grave was empty and that Jesus was alive (Matthew 28:1; John 19:25). It wasn't so much that he *didn't* believe her. He *couldn't* believe her. It just seemed impossible.

These men, in their confusion, were now encountering the One who had answers for their questions. And what impresses me about what follows is not only Jesus' concern that they be brought to understanding but also the patience with which He moved them forward in their faith—slowly, patiently, deliberately—the same way He works with us. Jesus did not choose a thunderbolt, but rather a still, small voice with which to instruct His disoriented friends.

The Confusion of the Disciples (vv. 21–24)

But we were hoping that it was He who was going to redeem Israel. Indeed, besides all this, it is the third day since these things happened. But also some women among us amazed us. When they were at the tomb early in the morning, and did not find His body, they came, saying that they had also seen a vision of angels who said that He was alive. Some of those who were with us went to the tomb and found it just exactly as the women also had said; but Him they did not see.

There is, I think, a distinct rawness to the emotions of these two heartbroken men. To their eyes, they were talking with a total stranger, yet they unburdened their souls and began to share their disappointment, and that disappointment was rooted and grounded in the confusion they felt over what had transpired. Do you hear them? "But we were hoping..." (v. 21). That is where the shoe pinches. That is where their hopes and expectations evolved into confusion. Things hadn't turned out as they thought. Their hopes were huge, and on that roller-coaster experience, the crash of those hopes would be equally huge. What was their expectation?

"But we were hoping that it was He who was going to redeem Israel" (Luke 24:21).

Since Genesis 3:15, following the spiritual failure of our first parents, the people of God had been waiting for the promised Rescuer. When God pronounced judgment on what one songwriter referred to as "the guilty pair bowed down with care," He also offered hope. God said to the deceiving serpent:

> "And I will put enmity between you and the woman, and between your seed and her seed; He shall bruise you on the head, and you shall bruise him on the heel" (Genesis 3:15).

The seed of the woman was the promise. One day a Rescuer would come. Along the way, the Old Testament had painted a series of pictures of the Deliverer who would come and even the forerunner who would precede Him (Malachi 3:1). When Jesus arrived, those hopes seemed to take on flesh. What was once only anticipation had become solid, objective, present. But now He was gone. And with Him, hope was gone.

Confusion is often the result when we are expecting certain things, when our hopes are high, but those hopes are left unrealized. To the Emmaus Road disciples' disappointment, however, was added new information that they simply did not know how to process. What happened? They recounted the latest rumors, things too unbelievable to be embraced as facts, and tried to match them up with Jesus' words and teachings:

- Some of the women had gone to the tomb and found it empty (including Mary, the wife of Cleopas). What could that mean?
- The women claimed to have seen angels bearing a message of resurrection. Is that even possible?
- Some of the men had gone to the tomb, and it was as the women had described—the body of Jesus was gone.
- Those men did not see Him, as the women had claimed to.

The last statement explains their despair. I suspect that in our hearts, all of us are Thomases. We doubt what we cannot see. We disbelieve what we cannot prove. I am convinced that, lacking concrete information to the contrary, we tend to fill in the blanks with assumption—and the assumptions tend to be negative.

The Emmaus Road disciples felt they had no concrete information to re-anchor their hopes, so they moved to the default position of doubt—"They did not see Him." So they found themselves walking away from Jerusalem and struggling with broken hearts and broken dreams. And confused.

Answers and Clarity

The longest chapter in the Bible (though technically not a chapter in the normal sense of the word) is Psalm 119. That great song is an anthem of praise to God for His Word, and it describes many remarkable things about the Scriptures, one of which is found in the declaration, "Your word is a lamp to my feet and a light to my path" (v. 105).

A lamp and a light are much needed comfort when we feel swallowed by the darkness around us. The Word of God, however, isn't a MagLite or a lighthouse or a search-light. The lamp spoken of here was a small, common olive oil lamp. It consisted of a clay bowl filled with oil and a small floating wick suspended in the liquid. When lit, it created light—but not much. Essentially, an olive oil lamp would produce just enough light for about one step. So, a person would proceed one step at a time using the limited light of the lamp to show the way.

The light of the Scriptures often has the same character-istics as an olive oil lamp. We want the Bible to be like the high beams of our car's headlights—clearing the darkness for as far as the eye can see. In our spiritual pilgrimage, however, we walk by faith, not by sight. With dependence upon the Holy Spirit and confidence in the light of the Word, we move forward—steady and determined but not reckless or foolish. It is in the wisdom of the Bible that we can find answers to our questions and clarity for our confusion—and it does this by giving us light for the next step of the way.

To these confused and struggling disciples, Jesus offered answers. Notice how Luke describes the scene:

And He said to them, "O foolish men and slow of heart to believe in all that the prophets have spoken! Was it not necessary for the Christ to suffer these things and to enter into His glory?" Then beginning with Moses and with all the prophets, He explained to them the things concerning Himself in all the Scriptures (Luke 24:25–27).

I have heard it said that this was, unquestionably, the greatest small group Bible study session ever held. The living Word of God, Jesus Christ, was expounding all the Old Testament Scriptures that pertained to Him. What might those have been? Luke doesn't tell us, but the teaching may have included:

- The promise of a Redeemer to crush the serpent's head (Genesis 3:15).
- The hope that, in order to redeem, God would become man (Isaiah 7:14; 9:6–7).
- The reality that this redemption would require the suffering and death of the God-man (Psalm 22; Isaiah 53).
- The fact that the grave would not be able to hold this conquering Savior (Job 19:25).

And that is just the low-hanging fruit for this discussion group. With the entire Old Testament at His disposal, the Master Rabbi explained to them all the Scriptures that had prophesied His coming, His work, His cross, and His victory. This remarkable exercise in the Word of God began to patch together understanding for their poor, confused minds. The power of the Word of God was beginning to move these men toward truth in a way they could never have hoped or imagined.

COMMUNION AND WONDER

> And they approached the village where they were going, and He acted as though He were going farther. But they urged Him, saying, "Stay with us, for it is getting toward evening, and the day is now nearly over." So He went in to stay with them (Luke 24:28–29).

Having been spiritually fed in such an extraordinary way, these men of Galilee didn't want the lesson to end! They encouraged the "anonymous" Jesus to stay with them, and at mealtime these two overwhelmed disciples sat down for dinner—unaware that the lessons begun in the Scriptures on the road would now find their zenith in the table before them. The unknown Traveler took full charge of the meal and, in a single act, opened their eyes as well as their understanding. Luke tells us:

> When He had reclined at the table with them, He took the bread and blessed it, and breaking it, He began giving it to them (Luke 24:30).

During those long dark days, while the followers of Christ were in hiding, we can only imagine how many times they had privately in their own hearts and corporately in their hushed conversations recounted the events of that tragic twenty-four hours that had so horrified their souls. The supper, then the garden. The arrest, then the trials. The cross, then the shame. The death, then the burial. Yet beginning it all was the trigger that had set those events in motion—the table. In the upper room Jesus had interrupted the paschal celebration and appropriated parts of the Passover into His own memorial feast, a feast that was launched as the King of heaven blessed and broke bread and then gave it to His men.

Now, in another room and in another town and at another table, the same Christ took bread and blessed it, broke it, and gave it to these two disciples. And in that moment, their worlds were transformed:

> Then their eyes were opened and they recognized Him; and He vanished from their sight (Luke 24:31).

In fact, what occurred in that flash of divine recognition was not one miracle but two. The miracle of Christ's resurrected body was once again demonstrated, as Jesus simply vanished. But while Christ's disappearance must have been a singularly powerful thing to witness, it wasn't what grabbed their attention the most. Their minds were pulled back into the walking Bible seminar they had experienced earlier that day. Their hearts were pulled back to the power of the Word of God.

They said to one another, "Were not our hearts burning within us while He was speaking to us on the road, while He was explaining the Scriptures to us?" (Luke 24:32).

It was the power of the Scriptures that demanded their attention—even in the face of the miraculous. Their description captures their extraordinary experience: their hearts afire as the Son of God explained the Word of God to them. The keys here are:

- *Burning hearts*—The idea of the word *burning* includes being overwhelmed and consumed.
- *Understanding minds*—The word *explaining*, in this context, according to *Strong's Exhaustive Concordance*, means "to open one's soul, i.e. to rouse in one the faculty of understanding or the desire of learning." To rouse, to stir, to provoke their minds—and to what? Understanding and the desire to learn!

The fact is that, unlike any other moment in their lives, they truly, deeply, personally *understood*. There is no substitute for understanding. As Proverbs says:

For if you cry for discernment, lift your voice for understanding... For the LORD gives wisdom; from His mouth come knowledge and understanding (2:3, 6).

For these two disciples, getting discernment, under-standing, and wisdom was not a theoretical concept. It was the flesh-and-bone experience of the Emmaus Road, and it was the tipping point both in their faith and their worldview from that day forward. Jesus was alive—the Scriptures were to be believed. Everything else took a backseat to that.

Following this marvelous scene, these two men who had earlier that day left Jerusalem in the slow walk of brokenhearted despair returned to the city excited and joy-filled. They had left overwhelmed with questions and had returned satisfied by the answers. They had left with uncertainty and confusion and had returned with clarity. The difference was made when the Shepherd of their hearts fed them the Word of God in a way that both satisfied their hearts and left them starving for more. It is in the heart that we experience and come to know the power of the Word of God.

So having seen the resurrection through the window of the Scriptures, we come back to my childhood church experi-ences. A sense of this extraordinary, marvelous, terrifying, awesome power of the Scriptures was what was missing. It was only years later, as a young adult, when I, for the first time, heard the message of the Savior with understanding that the power of the Word of God became real. In that moment, I could never again dismiss studying God's ancient book as an intellectual exercise. Coming to know the power of the Word of God must be seen as a soul-defining experience at the feet of the Master Teacher. It must be seen as the life-enriching privilege of drinking at a fountain of living waters. That Word must burn in our hearts.

Perhaps that is why in Bible college my homiletics professor hammered into his students, in his words, "It is a sin to make the Bible dull." To so minimize the power of the Bible is to deny the very message it contains. And that will never do. Instead, may it be said of us:

> For this reason we also constantly thank God that when you received the word of God which you heard from us, you accepted it not as the word of men, but for what it really is, the word of God, which also performs its work in you who believe (1 Thessalonians 2:13).

I pray we will listen with hearts ready to hear and that, like those men on the Emmaus Road, our hearts will burn within us as the powerful Word of the living God transforms our lives into the image of Christ.

OUR WINDOW *on* Easter

The men and women who witnessed the events surrounding the passion of Christ saw more than words could ever express. They heard things that, in some cases, we can only imagine. Their senses absorbed what we seek to grasp with hungry hearts and anxious minds.

But, at the end of the day, what they saw in history we have seen in the Scriptures—and the result is amazingly the same. The risen Lord, confronting the doubting disciple, Thomas, on his own turf, said, "Because you have seen Me, have you believed? Blessed are they who did not see, and yet believed" (John 20:29). Friends, the Savior was speaking of us! Though we may not have seen Him physically, we have seen Him through the pages of sacred writ and found good ground for belief. The book of Romans explains the phenomenon this way:

> So faith comes from hearing, and hearing by the word of Christ (10:17).

We have heard, and we have believed. But it mustn't end there. As the pair on the Emmaus Road experienced the faith of a burning heart, we too must burn with passion to know Him—the very passion of the apostle Paul, who wrote that his life's goal was, "that I may know Him and the power of His resurrection and the fellowship of His sufferings, being conformed to His death" (Philippians 3:10).

May that same desire burn in our hearts as well, that we might truly know the One who loved us and gave himself for us.

NOTE TO THE READER

The publisher invites you to share your response to the message of this book by writing Discovery House, P.O. Box 3566, Grand Rapids, MI 49501, USA. For information about other Discovery House books, music, or DVDs, contact us at the same address or call 1–800–653–8333. Find us online at dhp.org or send e-mail to books@dhp.org.